CONTENTS

THE ETHNOGRAPHER'S METHOD

ALEX STEWART
Texas Tech University

Qualitative Research Methods
Volume 46

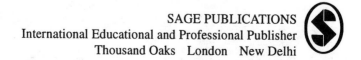

SAGE PUBLICATIONS
International Educational and Professional Publisher
Thousand Oaks   London   New Delhi

For information:

SAGE Publications, Inc.
2455 Teller Road
Thousand Oaks, California 91320
E-mail: order@sagepub.com

SAGE Publications Ltd.
6 Bonhill Street
London EC2A 4PU
United Kingdom

SAGE Publications India Pvt. Ltd.
M-32 Market
Greater Kailash I
New Delhi 110 048 India

Printed in the United States of America

Library of Congress Cataloging-in-Publication Data

Stewart, Alex.
    The ethnographer's method / by Alex Stewart.
        p. cm. — (Qualitative research methods; v. 46)
    Includes bibliographical references.
    ISBN 0-7619-0393-3 (cloth: acid-free paper)
    ISBN 0-7619-0394-1 (pbk.: acid-free paper)
    1. Ethnology—Field work. 2. Participant observation.
    3. Ethnology—Methodology. I. Title. II. Series.
    GN346.S74 1998
    305.8'007'23—ddc21
                                          98-8904
                                             CIP

98 99 00 01 02 03 04 10 9 8 7 6 5 4 3 2 1

Acquiring Editor:	Peter Labella
Editorial Assistant:	Corinne Pierce
Production Editor:	Michèle Lingre
Production Assistant:	Denise Santoyo
Typesetter:	Marion Warren

SERIES EDITORS' INTRODUCTION

Qualitative research is an ethnographic process. Generally, the field-worker—whether trained in cultural anthropology, sociology, political science, or another social science—seeks to develop insights about a targeted culture by practicing some form of participant observation. It is the convention to report research results in an ethnographic volume, article, or report. Of course, this tidy explanation masks the fact that ethnographies can differ dramatically from one another in theoretical orientation, scope, technique of data collection, degree of quantitative analysis, and audience, among many other dimensions by which research might be coded. Although it may be appealing to announce that ethnographies exhibit a great diversity of forms, we ought also to worry that a lack of attention to standards could create a situation in which *any* form is given ethnographic legitimacy.

In this 46th volume of Sage's **Qualitative Research Methods** Series, Alex Stewart raises the difficult and important question of how we can tell if a particular ethnography is good work or not. The answer he provides has several components. First, the ethnographic product must be faithful to the truth, or successful in its "depiction". Second, the ethnography must communicate conclusions that can be shown to "transcend" the perspectives of the individual researcher. Finally, the ethnography must generate understandings that are "applicable" to the study of human behavior in other research settings.

Stewart very deliberately instructs us how familiar issues of validity are incorporated in a concern for "veracity," how issues of reliability are reflected in those of "objectivity," and how issues of generalizability are encompassed in attention to "perspicacity." In doing this, he strives to create a framework for evaluation that is meaningful not only for qualitative researchers who view their work as scientific, but also for those who are committed to producing postmodern, poetic, and other nonscientific ethnographies.

—Marc L. Miller
Peter K. Manning
John Van Maanen

ACKNOWLEDGMENTS

Many thanks to my wife, Marjory, and my children, Ben, Ian, and Arden, who worked hard to make the time for this effort. Carlton Whitehead worked hard to make the professional space for my work. Considering that nobody before me had been so audacious as to do a book on ethnographic method discussions, you could rightly assume it was a pretty unusual space. This book is dedicated to him. John Van Maanen, despite his documented differences with some of the positions I advance, encouraged this project from the start and made timely and canny comments. For their helpful comments I also thank Shelby Hunt, Marc Miller, Bill Stein, and Harry Wolcott. The usual caveats apply.

ARTICULATING ETHNOGRAPHIC METHOD

ALEX STEWART
Texas Tech University

1. WHO WILL DETERMINE EXPECTATIONS?

Why Write a Book on Ethnographic Method Discussions?

Confessional introduction. I think I have read enough ethnographies, and tried my hand enough myself, that I understand the ethnographic method writings when I read them. But that literature, and not my personal abilities, is the warrant I present for preparing this book.[1] Now, if I aver such humility, how (one may ask) could I have written a book with such a presumptuous mandate? Like so much in ethnography (and life), it was an accident. As a probationary novice (i.e., assistant professor) in a research-dominated business school, I wanted to submit my studies to the major management journals. But those journals generally seemed not to know what to expect of an ethnography. The case studies they sometimes published typically cited, glibly and ceremonially, Glaser and Strauss (1967), occasionally Miles and Huberman (1984), or Yin (1984; see Aldrich, Fowler, Liou, & Marsh, 1994). Authors would say, for example, "We used the method of Miles and Huberman (1984)." This is about as helpful as a multivariate study specified merely by the offhand, "We used the method of Blalock (1967)." Accordingly, I set to work writing a method appendix that would not only specify *what* I had done, but also *why* this was what I should specify. The manuscript mushroomed to the point that I realized that I was creating a testimony for a wider audience—that I was at work on this book.

Audiences for this book. This allegation of a wider audience (so obviously self-promoting) is based on the view that a framework for discussing ethnographic method would be helpful for four audiences. If this book is to explain ethnographers' method discussions—that is, articulate how they articulate their method—it must, in the same breath, explain their research design. Research design is the method discussion viewed from the start; method discussion is research design viewed from the finish. For this reason, the first audience is beginning ethnographers. The second audience is ethnographers hoping for funding, or for positive reviews by the nonethnographic journals. The third audience is reviewers for funding bodies and journals. (Reviewers for monograph houses and for journals in anthropology and sociology can be taken to be knowledgeable judges of ethnographic method. However, even in these fields there is little consensus on what should constitute an ethnographic method discussion.)[2] The fourth audience is any scholars, untrained in ethnographic method, who would like to be able to assess the research method footings of the ethnographies that they read.

Should Ethnographers Write Method Discussions?

UNDERDEVELOPED DISCUSSIONS

Norms about method discussions for ethnography are underdeveloped, even in the discipline that first developed such inquiry: anthropology. It would be hard to accuse anthropological ethnographers of that obsession with method that Janesick (1994) decries as "methodolatry." [3] If one looks for research method discussions in the leading anthropology journals (e.g., *American Ethnologist, Man/Journal of the Royal Anthropological Institute*), one will, by and large, come up empty. In the more sociologically rooted journals that routinely publish ethnography (e.g., *Journal of Contemporary Ethnography, Qualitative Sociology*), method is discussed, but briefly. Articles seldom explain the character or the management of the data. Method discussions in applied social science are more fully formed, but not well tailored to ethnography. Because the applied journals publish few ethnographies, relative to grounded theories, naturalistic inquiries, and rapid appraisals, the expectations that may be forming are likely nonethnographic. Discussions focus on concerns, such as rater reliability checks, that are much less important in ethnography than, say, the observer's relations with the actors.

Method discussions are less rare in ethnographic books than in ethnographic articles. Malinowski's (1922/1961) introduction to *Argonauts of the Western Pacific* is the celebrated ancestor of the various appendices, forewords, afterwords, and incidental writings of this genre (Stocking, 1992). However, one can search shelf after shelf of ethnographic books and find few if any of these discussions. One reason for this methodological silence is that "by far the most prominent, familiar, prevalent, popular, and recognized form of ethnographic writing is the realist account" (Van Maanen, 1988, p. 45). In this tradition, one should get on with depiction and with theory, and not break stride to bother about how the ethnographer came to acquire that knowledge. Even today, it is hard to disagree with Burridge (1960), who in a prologue noted that "when in the field anthropologists frequently have experiences which they tend to reserve for dinner parties or as a relaxation after seminars. Only rarely do such anecdotes find their way into serious discourse" (p. 1).

REASONS NOT TO DISCUSS
ETHNOGRAPHIC METHOD

Could it be that methodological reticence is a warning against the project of this book? Perhaps a research method discussion in ethnography would be but an artificial graft, tacked on only to pacify reviewers, of grant proposals and manuscript submissions, in disciplines that mandate such inscriptions (Sanjek, 1991). Method discussion might lack value outside the publish-or-perish games that are notorious in "Nacirema" academic culture.[4] After all, the formalization of ethnographic method is radically limited, by the flexibility of the investigative process and by the uniqueness of each research situation. Moreover, anthropologists revel in their distinctiveness, viewing themselves as "rugged individuals" (Jackson, 1990, p. 32). As Wolcott (1992) has confessed of qualitative scholars, "We are all self-styled researchers" (p. 39; emphasis removed).[5]

If ethnographic practice truly is idiosyncratic, only its outcomes can be evaluated. Thus, "for anthropologists, ethnography is not a method; it is a product" (Muecke, 1994, p. 190). Statistically oriented researchers may use "methodological rigor" to "convince" their readers, but ethnographers use different means (Golden-Biddle & Locke, 1993, p. 597). Moreover, they seek different ends: In ethnography, data and analysis pale in importance compared to the goal of generating insight.[6]

In some views, only the most rudimentary norms may be prescribed for the method for achieving this goal—to wit, one does need to think about data; this thinking cannot be speeded up (Wolcott, 1994, pp. 37, 39). But it matters not at all just how interpretations are derived, because the "brief bursts of insight or pattern recognition" (Wolcott, 1994, p. 24) that are the wellsprings of true understanding use imagination to "transcend" the data (Asad, 1994; Whyte, 1984, p. 21; Wolcott, 1994, p. 258). Thus, "like poems and hypotheses, ethnographies can only be judged *ex post,* after someone has brought them into being" (Geertz, 1988, p. 147).

REASONS TO DISCUSS ETHNOGRAPHIC METHOD

Anthropologists do have their reasons for paying so little attention to describing research method. However, there are reasons to be a great deal more explicit. From the reader's perspective, discussion of method allows for a more informed judgment about which aspects of the study to accept, to reject, and to qualify (Agar, 1996, p. 14). Further, "if one is committed to *application* of knowledge as well as its creation, one needs credible arguments to persuade skeptical people who are being asked to put themselves on the line" (Agar, 1996, p. 15). No matter how long the report, no matter how tireless the reader, the data as presented must be partial—more partial than what the ethnographer knows (Agar, 1996, pp. 38-39). They are seldom little more than "apt illustrations" (Gluckman, 1961). The reader needs more than these illustrations in order to judge just how apt they really are (Wolcott, 1990b, p. 27).[7]

Another benefit of explicit discussion of method would be guidance in the training of novice ethnographers. Would-be ethnographers who lack much background in anthropology, or ethnographic sociology, could be helped by such discussions. Whether or not such people ought to try their hands at ethnography, prior to disciplinary training, is another quite debatable question (Wolcott, 1990a, 1992). The ethnographic mistrust of methodology is entirely justified, insofar as methodology becomes a replacement for disciplinary training (compare Wolcott, 1994, p. 35). Still, method discussions could help to motivate better studies. If ethnographers were aware, when they did their research, that they would be held accountable on methodological grounds, they might make better methodological decisions (for example, spend more time in the field) (Schwandt & Halpern, 1988). Moreover, better-developed norms about method discussions could help ethnographers get their papers published, by means of better explanations of method to certain reviewers or other readers who might not be well acquainted with ethnography.

Readers who become more familiar with ethnographic method become more discerning, and (hopefully) more sympathetic. Perhaps this is why Wolcott (1990a) holds that "anyone who engages in ethnography also assumes responsibility to participate in . . . seeking satisfactory ways to explain ethnography to others" (p. 47). If ethnography had its own norms of explanation, it would be freer from the methodological norms of other research traditions, such as those developed in economics and psychology. So long as it lacks its own norms, ethnography submitted for publication in most nonanthropological journals will continue to be evaluated according to criteria developed for statistics-oriented research.[8] Readers, reviewers included, do have expectations about method, whether or not ethnographers write method discussions. If ethnographers articulate their own mode of method discussions, these expectations could be *for,* not just *about* their research.

2. DEPICTING ETHNOGRAPHIC METHOD

Subjecting ethnography to the methodological standards of psychometrics or econometrics is hardly appropriate. Subjecting it to the standards of other qualitative methods might be a little better. Grounded theory and naturalistic inquiry are alternative qualitative, case study methods that are especially liable to affect reviewing standards, because, unlike ethnography, they have explicit methods standards. Shortly, it will be shown that their influence could lead to misunderstandings for ethnographers.

What Is Ethnographic Research?

If ethnography is not the same as other case or qualitative research methods, what is it? There is no universally adopted definition that one can appropriate, likely because there are many forms of ethnographic research (Boyle, 1994; Wolcott, 1992). Therefore, the meaning used for this book must be clarified. To do this, I propose that this research has four characteristics that are widely accepted, and a fifth that ought, perhaps, to be added. The proposed definition is not intended as essentialist, due to a lesson of taxonomy (McKelvey, 1982; Needham, 1975), that empirical boundaries between social taxa are typically polythetic. Thus, there may be *no* features (e.g., participant observation, contextualism, interpretation) that, by their presence, entirely assign a study to a category or taxon. Moreover, specialized forms of ethnography (such as analytic ethnography; Lofland, 1995) may have additional diacritical criteria, which are left to their proponents to explain.

Participant observation. The first characteristic of an ethnographic study is participant observation. Ethnography shares with certain other modes of field studies (e.g., ethnomethodology) the up-close involvement of the researcher in some form of participative role, in the natural, "everyday" setting to be studied. Multiple approaches to data collection are deployed (Asad, 1994; Hammersley, 1990), but there is one focal research instrument. That so-called instrument is the ethnographer's own inquiring experience, in joint, emergent exploration with people who once were called *natives*—but let us style them here either as *actors* or *insiders.*[9]

Holism. The second characteristic of ethnography, which follows from the first, is a holistic mandate. Of the various possible senses of the term *holism* (Johnson & Johnson, 1990), two are vital. The first is that the ethnographer synthesizes disparate observations to create a holistic construct of "culture" or "society" (Strathern, 1992; Thornton, 1988). According to this sense, the "enduring core meaning of holism for anthropology [is] that culture [or society] is an integrated whole and that individuals can only be understood within the context of that whole" (Johnson & Johnson, 1990, p. 167). The second sense is that the range of attention is "comprehensive" (Johnson, 1987). Good ethnographic data are wide-ranging; they have, in Becker's (1996, p. 65) expression, "breadth."

Comprehensiveness is limited in practice and in fashions.[10] There is little doubt that writings based on ethnographic research—especially journal articles—cannot be all-embracing (Adler & Adler, 1995). Nor is traditional comprehensiveness in fashion (Agar, 1996, p. 4). Comprehensiveness had been justified by totalizing concepts, such as culture, whose ontological status is no longer clear (Strathern, 1992; Thornton, 1988). The trend in ethnographic writing is away from comprehensiveness and toward narrower focus (Johnson, 1987). With these caveats, it is still true that the range of observations transcends academic disciplines and specialties. This, rather limited, meaning of holism persists as a distinguishing feature of ethnography.

Context sensitivity. The third characteristic of ethnography, which follows from the first and the second, is contextualized explanation. Immersion within a particular setting leads the ethnographer to see linkages among various strands in holistic—that is, comprehensive—data. Ethnographers explain one set of observations in terms of connections with others, and with concepts used for their fit with the context (Agar, 1986b). Some ethnographic explanations are abstracted from the range of social life observed, but even these must closely shadow the specifics of the site. "Ethnographers usually prefer a model of complex, unique systems subject to situational logic, interpretation, and narration" (Van Maanen, 1988, p. 43).[11] This is the approach that makes sense to them, that matches their immersion in "local conditions as an experiential whole" (Asad, 1994, p. 57). Due to spatial and temporal limits on fieldwork, "the traditional ethnographic concern for context" (Wolcott, 1994, p. 30) may be limited somewhat to the context that is locally observable (however, see Burawoy, 1991; Firth, 1977; Lyon, 1997). Nonetheless, contextualism as an ideal has been dominant methodologically since the days of Malinowski (Strathern, 1987).

Sociocultural description. The fourth characteristic of ethnography, which follows from personal involvement in human contexts, is the detailed depiction and analysis of social relations and culture (Wolcott, 1992, p. 27). Ethnography's domain is, in Wolcott's (1992, p. 42) unexceptionable term, "sociocultural." In his more controversial term, explanation, to be ethnographic, must be "cultural" (Wolcott, 1990a, 1992; see also Rosen, 1991; Van Maanen, 1988, p. 1). This term reflects the position of U.S. cultural anthropology. British school social anthropologists hold that "the dialectic between culture and society is weighted in the opposite direction" (Lewis, 1976, p. 19; see also Beattie, 1966, pp. 20-21).[12] Regardless of their emphasis, ethnographers agree that culture matters, at least in the sense that the ethnographer records the "subjective vision" of the actors (Asad, 1994, p. 57).[13] The charter myth statement is Malinowski's (1922/ 1961): "The final goal, of which an Ethnographer should never lose sight . . . is . . . to grasp the native's point of view" (p. 25; see also pp. 19, 22-24).

Theoretical connections. A fifth, contestable, characteristic of ethnography is the use of anthropological (or sociological) theory. The question is whether, absent this theory, a study can truly be ethnographic. Trotter (1991, p. 180) has argued (as has Rosen, 1991) that ethnography requires "the framework of anthropological theory." A problem with this position is that theory and ethnography, as methods, have had separate histories within anthropology (Stocking, 1992, p. 58; Van Maanen, 1995). As Fardon (1990) points out, 20th-century anthropology has seen successive waves of theories, but only one watershed of method, the rise of ethnography based on participant observation. (This seems to be the basis of Wolcott's [1990b, p. 26] argument in favor of very short method discussions: It's all old hat.)

The timelessness of ethnography, *qua* method, is held to mean that an ethnographic study makes a contribution that transcends the theory it espouses (Johnson, 1987). It is also held that an ethnographic study, if it is to make a contribution, must espouse some theory, whatever the provenance of that theory may be (Adler & Adler, 1995). A strong version of this requirement, voiced in anthropology, is that "new concepts have to exist at the end of the study that didn't exist in the original research problem" (Agar, 1996, p. 39). A weaker version of this requirement, voiced in sociology, is that an ethnography helps us reconsider, or "reconstruct," interesting theories (Burawoy, 1991; see also the anthropologist Wolcott, 1994, p. 45). Theory matters, then, but ethnography is not as focused on theory, or on concepts, as is grounded theory.

ETHNOGRAPHY ≈ GROUNDED THEORY
(BUT IT ISN'T THE SAME)

In applied social research (at least in education, health, and management), the nonethnographic qualitative method that is prominent—and hence likely to influence reviewers' expectations—is grounded theory. *The Discovery of Grounded Theory* (Glaser & Strauss, 1967) has often been used "in a rhetoric of justification . . . [as] a superficial and hollow stamp of approval" (Locke, 1996, p. 244). For example, in the field of management, ethnographies are much less common than grounded theories (Locke, 1996). It is not surprising, then, that in certain fields "the 'grounded theory' tradition . . . is often, in our view mistakenly, presented as the dominant approach to theorizing in qualitative research" (Richards & Richards, 1994, p. 446). This mistake is not discouraged by generic-sounding titles like *Basics of Qualitative Research* (Strauss & Corbin, 1990).

Common ground. Grounded theory and ethnography do share common ground.[14] They both use comparable processes of generating understanding with iterative comparisons of data and theory (Agar, 1986b, pp. 16, 25-27).

Further, ethnographic theory is "grounded," as ethnographers prioritize trying to think through observations in the terms of their immanent context, before trying to construe the data in the light of existing theories.[15]

Differences. Nonetheless, the ethnographic process is distinctive. The modernist comparative method (at least in anthropology, since Malinowski) has been a "comparison of distinct systems," "a comparison of contexts" (Strathern, 1987, pp. 254, 261). Although some ethnography has been criticized for the quickness of its leap to abstraction (Wikan, 1991), the normative orientation is reflected by Wolcott's (1994) advice to focus on description, compared to analysis or interpretation. This orientation is shared by ethnographers and by other, nonethnographic, case researchers.[16] It is not shared by grounded theory.

Grounded theory has at least two attractions that ethnography lacks. In grounded theory, methodological procedures are documented in detail, most notably in a volume with another generic-sounding title, *Qualitative Analysis for Social Scientists* (Strauss, 1987). The time demands for grounded theory must also be very attractive to contract researchers and publish-or-perish-pressured authors. For example, Strauss (1987) has asserted that "one doesn't have to spend a lot of time and energy in the typical fieldworker's fashion, because theoretical sampling [for grounded theory] allows for more efficient, short-time observation and interviewing" (p. 275). More efficient, that is, if one cares about concepts, but not about context.

The key word in grounded theory is *theory,* not *grounded.* Its protocol prescribes the coding of "context" or "conditions" (Strauss, 1987; Strauss & Corbin, 1990), but by ethnographic standards the "constant comparisons" are seldom directed at the data (Emerson, Fretz, & Shaw, 1995, p. 167). Comparisons become abstracted from specifics, such as the particular actors, to concepts, where most of the efforts are focused (Strauss, 1987, pp. 20-21, 32, 127-128). Consequently, "grounded theory represses the specificity of each situation" (Burawoy, 1991, p. 271).

The distinction between this approach and that of ethnography is illustrated by the contrast between a classic book, of which Strauss is the fourth author, and a more recent book of which he is the first of four. *Boys in White: Student Culture in Medical School* (Becker, Geer, Hughes, & Strauss, 1961) is a study of a particular medical school (University of Kansas), organized throughout by the progress of students through their studies. *Social Organization of Medical Work* (Strauss, Fagerhaugh, Suczek, & Wiener, 1985) is a study of the generic hospital, organized throughout by conceptual topics, such as "machine work" and "safety work." The first book is ethnography; the second, grounded theory.

ETHNOGRAPHY ≈ NATURALISTIC INQUIRY (BUT IT ISN'T THE SAME)

In other applied fields (such as education and marketing), naturalistic inquiry is an influential nonethnographic approach to qualitative research. Naturalistic inquiry, like grounded theory, has the attraction of an explicit canon of standards (Guba, 1981; Lincoln & Guba, 1986, 1990). Possibly ethnographers should borrow this attraction by adopting the naturalistic canon as their own. The view that those expectations also apply to ethnography seems to be taken by Wallendorf and Belk (1989) and by Gliner (1994).[17] And why not, for surely naturalistic inquiry is close enough to ethnography that one could write an ethnography and present it as a naturalistic inquiry. How distinctive could ethnographic standards really be? As distinctive as participant observation, which is central to ethnography, but peripheral to naturalistic inquiry.

Guba's (1981) "Criteria for Assessing the Trustworthiness of Naturalistic Inquiries" is the foundational statement of expectations for this method. This statement omits considerations of site selection, as well as the participant observer role and closely related topics such as the ethnographer's path, speech-in-action, and the field conditions affecting informant statements. These will be shown to be focal concerns for ethnographic method. Guba (1981) also recommends research method tactics—stepwise replication and audit trails—that are decidedly nonethnographic.[18]

How Could Ethnographic Method Be Depicted?

CRITERIA AND STANDARDS FOR JUDGING ETHNOGRAPHIC METHOD

A gap in the literature. If one decides that an ethnographic "method" section would be useful, and distinct from cognate discussions, one needs to settle on the criteria for ethnographic method. Adler and Adler (1995) may well be correct that judgments of the quality of ethnographies, taken as wholes, are based on "established norms and guidelines" (p. 20). However, consensus does not extend to expectations about method discussions. As Lofland and Lofland (1995) observe, "The character and content of methodological accounts are not highly standardized" (p. 222).[19] One aspect of actual ethnographic practice—thinking about and using field notes—has been researched by Jackson (1990). Her interviews with 70 field researchers uncovered a "lack of standard methodology" and of knowledge of "the methodological canons" (p. 26). To the best of my knowledge, no empirical study directly addresses how ethnographic readers and reviewers utilize methods criteria. Extrapolating from research in other fields would suggest that the reliability of reviews will be low, and agreement on criteria will be "modest" at best (Campion, 1993a, p. 32; Cicchetti, 1991).

UNIQUE OR PARALLEL CRITERIA?

Using criteria that "parallel" those of statistics-oriented research (Guba, 1981) would foster scholarly standardization, which does have its benefits. As Markus (1992) has argued, the use of common approaches, such as the standard article format, facilitates dialogue across research styles and scholarly specialties. Moreover, what is good for knowledge in general may also be good for ethnography in particular. If ethnographers ask that a gatekeeper, trained in another tradition, review their work by standards that could appear self-serving, it is doubtful that they will get a sympathetic ear (Becker, 1996). If they ask to be judged by standards that are merely custom-fitted versions of off-the-rack approaches, their odds will be greatly improved.

Limitations of statistics-oriented terminology. However, if there is one point of terminological concord among ethnographers, it is the folly of applying to their research, with no qualification or translation, the expectations of statistics-oriented research (Leininger, 1994). Certainly, it is tough to apply the edicts of the "Method" section of the *Publication Manual of the American Psychological Association,* with its focus on full replicability and concerns for "procedure" and "apparatus" (or "materials") (American Psychological Association, 1994, pp. 12-15). Another case in point is an "Article Review Checklist" for applied psychology, the guidelines of which for "qualitative" research—for example, "[ensure that the work] describes procedural details fully, such that replication is possible" (Campion, 1993b, p. 714)—are heavily slanted toward statistics-oriented research. The prescriptions, such as "[ensure that the author] conducts content analysis correctly" (Campion 1993b, p. 714), are also too abstract to provide any guidance for researchers.

Frustration with the inappropriateness, for ethnography, of statistics-oriented standards has prompted proposals for specifically suitable language. It has also inspired terminological innovations. For example, Van Maanen (1988) proposes the criteria of "apparency and verisimilitude" (p. xi); Hammersley (1990) proposes "plausibility" and "credibility" (pp. 61-62); Golden-Biddle and Locke (1993) propose "plausibility," "authenticity," and "criticality"; and Leininger (1994) proposes "credibility," "confirmability," "meaning-in-context," "recurrent patterning," "saturation," and "transferability."

Lincoln and Guba (1986) call these sorts of criteria, which refer in the first instance to qualitative research, "unique," as opposed to "parallel" (p. 78). A good case has been made on behalf of unique criteria, for their fit with epistemological assumptions (Fabian, 1991; Leininger, 1994). Conventional terminology, by contrast, carries connotations that extend well beyond epistemic values into the expected research tactics, especially those that focus on measurement and statistical inference. Ethnographic research tactics differ so markedly that ethnographies also differ in the substance of the findings. Thus, another advantage of unique criteria is an unblinkered focus on issues often neglected in statistics-oriented research. One such issue is the set of ethical, fieldwork, and rhetorical challenges of articulating the multiple perspectives of stakeholders in a study. This issue appears to underlie Lincoln and Guba's (1986) "authenticity" criteria.

A daunting impediment to the use of such unique criteria is that they are, as yet, conceptually underdeveloped (Lincoln & Guba, 1986). Because of this underspecification, and the advantages of using standardized models, parallel criteria are attractive. Therefore, for this book I borrow Guba's (1981) approach to adopting a middle position. This approach proposes, to the extent that is required, unique criteria that, to the extent that is befitting, parallel conventional concepts.

Truth as the Ultimate Objective

Statistics-oriented researchers and ethnographers share an ultimate epistemic value. Whether or not they define themselves as "scientists," they both adhere to the fundamental purpose of science: to try to learn the truth about the world. Lofland and Lofland (1995, pp. 74, 150) and LeCompte and Preissle (1993, p. 315), for example, advocate this purpose for ethnography. Certainly, it is difficult to see why people would put up with the tribulations of participant observation, would bother to *be there*, if they did not hope that their accounts would be more or less true.[20]

POSTMODERNIST CRITIQUES
OF TRUTH AS A GOAL

It is, however, a well-publicized fact that some ethnographers disdain the pursuit of scientific knowledge, regarding this goal as the mark of, at best, naïveté. One of the editors of this book series, for example, has written that "the cry of science is less popular now and the perspective and style of the ethnographies that fly its flag are dated, reflecting a naive era that is no longer epistemologically viable or socially defensible" (Van Maanen, 1995, p. 73). This perspective is, stereotypically, postmodernist.

Postmodernists assert that there are "multiple realities," because they believe, or write as if they believe, that cultures and mental representations equal reality (e.g., Lincoln & Denzin, 1994). For example, Emerson et al. (1995, pp. 3, 11-12), in a perceptive text on field notes, make an unassailable observation, that researchers cannot gain privileged access to "the truth," deriving an unassailable conclusion, that researchers ought to minimize the partiality of their perspectives by seeking out multiple members' perspectives. So far, so good. But on these epistemological and methodological bases, they slide into an ontology, in which actors' perspectives become "truths" and the ethnographer's purpose is to comprehend these multiple truths.

If it is conceded that postmodernist writing can demonstrate access to multiple representations of reality—a humanly limited number of these— there still remains the question of how this knowledge was obtained. Surely it was by the method that was used. Method is the means to help learn about the world, and not just any world, the "real" world. This latter purpose is not *empirically* required. Rather, a realist ontology is a necessary condition, or "presupposition," of the intelligibility of discourse (Searle, 1995, p. 182) and (it follows) of ethnography. Further, it is a presupposition if one is to have any business writing research method discussions (Hammersley, 1990, p. 61; Hunt, 1990, 1991, pp. 379-380). Otherwise one merely pretends, pandering to norms at odds with one's ontological stance.

There is a discrepancy in postmodernist naturalistic inquiry between, on one hand, method prescriptions such as interrater checks and audit trails, and on the other hand, the antirealist ontology proclaimed (Lincoln & Guba, 1986, 1990; compare Abbott's commentary in Aunger, 1995; Agar, 1996, p. 51). Postmodernism has contributed to ethnographic method by sensitizing readers to the multiplicity of perspectives, including those of the ethnographers, in research settings (see the discussion of the ethnographer's path in Chapter 4). However, the problem with postmodernism

14

comes down to this: The multiple realities that are asserted are not that, but rather multiple representations, each based on the limited purchase that one mind can have upon truth about reality. They have an epistemic, not an ontological, status. Postmodernism thus commits the antirealist fallacy of trying "to derive conclusions about reality from features of our representations of reality" (Searle, 1995, p. 159; also generally Chapters 7, 8; see also D'Andrade, 1995).[21]

TRUTH AS A LEGITIMATE RESEARCH GOAL

Truth is, after all, a legitimate target. But what precisely is it? Following Ellis (1990), truth is a mode of epistemic evaluation, and the outcome of that evaluation. It is what is right to believe, based upon our epistemic values. When our concern is research method, these epistemic values are the values of science. Scientific values are not the only legitimate values, and the measures of truth that are gained from their guidance are not the only truths offered in ethnography. An ethnographer might, for example, manage to reveal a moral truth, an artistic truth, or perhaps—if this appears conceivable—a religious truth. But none of these truths is the concern of research method. When research method is at issue, as in this book, truth is what is right to believe, provisionally and critically, based upon our best means of understanding the reality of the subject at hand (Hunt, 1990).

ADAPTING CONVENTIONAL CRITERIA

To the extent that ethnography shares this goal—to learn, the best it can, some glimmerings of truth about the world—the epistemic values of scientific research are also those of ethnography. If we grant the contention of conventional researchers (e.g., Babbie, 1983) that well-developed, statistics-oriented criteria—validity, reliability, and generalizability—are scientific, it follows that ethnographers should show the connections between these and their own criteria. Shared epistemic values would justify the parallels; distinctive obstacles and tactics—research pragmatics— would justify tailoring of standards. This is the rationale that Guba (1981) presents in his proposed terms for criteria that parallel those of conventional research, but also connote the pragmatics of naturalistic inquiry. This book attempts to do the same for ethnography.

From validity to veracity. Validity appears to be a criterion that transfers over slickly from statistics-oriented method (Kirk & Miller, 1986; Sanjek, 1990a). Wolcott (1994), however, argues persuasively that this criterion is overly laden with connotations of measurement, psychometrics, and external validity or generalizability. In statistics-oriented studies, validity raises the question, Has one measured just what it is one thinks one has? The pertinent question for ethnographers is not whether they have measured what they think they have, but rather (Lofland, 1995; Wolcott, 1994), Have they really observed what their descriptions claim? Have they achieved "verisimilitude" (Van Maanen, 1988, p. xi)? For this criterion, the word I adopt in this volume is *veracity,* which (according to *Merriam-Webster's Collegiate Dictionary,* 10th edition) means "**1**: devotion to the truth . . . **2**: power of conveying or perceiving truth . . . **3**: conformity with truth or fact." The second meaning might appear attuned to empathic understanding, and hence the most ethnographic, but the first and third meanings are also fundamental for ethnographic method (see Chapter 3). The pivotal question raised by veracity is, How well, with what verisimilitude, does this study succeed in its *depiction*?

From reliability to objectivity. The conventional value of reliability raises multiple questions. Are the measurements unbiased and free from observer effects? Are they replicable? Are they stable? The first two questions are at odds with participant observation, which involves observer effects and cannot be replicated literally (Hammersley, 1990, p. 61). Ethnography is also a mode of continuous learning about topics—people, their cultures, their relationships—that are themselves in flux (Ottenberg, 1990, 1994; Van Maanen, 1991). Moreover, reports by informants are inherently "highly situational" (Dean & Whyte, 1958, p. 35; emphasis removed). There is no reason to assume "that there is invariably some basic underlying attitude or opinion that a person is firmly [i.e., consistently] committed to" (Dean & Whyte, 1958, p. 35). Stability or consistency would be both a misguided and an impossible objective for ethnography.[22]

Despite these differences between statistical and ethnographic research, there is a fundamental question that is central to both. Ethnographers, even more than conventional researchers, deal in one of the ways in which people can overcome the limited purchase of any particular perspective on the world. They act and speak with others. Their inquiry is at root an effort at intersubjective, often intercultural, communication. In this fundamental sense it profoundly aspires to objectivity, in the sense of intersubjectivity (Fabian, 1991). Moreover, Boon (1995) asserts, cultural anthropologists aspire more hopefully still toward " 'ultraobjectivity,' or, following *Webster's,* that which is 'intersubjectively observable' . . . 'beyond what is ordinary' " (p. 180). The ethnographer's aspiration is to make a claim that "holds not just for me (egocentric subjectivity) or for some of us (parochial subjectivity) but for all of us (impersonal or interpersonal objectivity)" (Rescher, 1997, p. 4; see also Hunt, 1991, pp. 51, 165, 197, 291; Searle, 1995, pp. 8-12). Objectivity, in the sense of the word that is used in this book, is related to values of alertness, receptivity to the views of others, empathy, and open-mindedness.[23] The pivotal question is, thus, How well does this study *transcend* the perspectives of the researcher? A corollary question is, How well does this study transcend the perspectives of informants?

From generalizability to perspicacity. The conventional value of generalizability raises the question, Are the measurements applicable to a population beyond the sample? If one understands generalizability in terms of samples and populations, the quest for generalizability will be as futile as the quest for conventional reliability. However, the question can be refocused on the extent to which ethnographers can develop a construct or theory, about structures, processes, or relationships, that is specified sufficiently so as to be applied beyond the site of the research. Ethnographic efforts to generalize begin with abstraction and finish by specifying the social, cultural, and temporal contingencies for which the findings apply. This effort relies on the efficacy of the analysis and theory construction. In order to reflect this distinctly ethnographic mode of transferring findings beyond the site of observations, a distinctly ethnographic term is needed.

The term for this criterion that I will use in this book is *perspicacity*. The first question raised by perspicacity is, Is this study revelatory? Assuming that the study has achieved some insight, the pivotal question, most relevant for research method discussions, is, Does this research generate *insights that are also applicable* to other times, other places, in the human experience? A question that could be taken to subsume both of these is, How fundamentally does this study explain?

Consensus on particular terms, such as *veracity, perspicacity,* and *objectivity,* may facilitate communication. However, terminology itself does not improve ethnographic practice. Only the effort to contend with the epistemic values to which these terms refer can improve the enterprise. My hope is that innovations and improvements in inquiry will be spurred by the recognition of our current limitations, and by the identification of both appropriate criteria and tactics that serve these criteria in ethnographic practice. Failure to make this effort, regardless of the language that is favored, would damage it. Veracity, objectivity, and perspicacity are values that cannot simply be defined or wished away.

Table 2.1 gives a sense of what it means to adopt this terminology. Expectations for ethnographic method comprise particular criteria and standards. Method is to be judged by a set of three criteria, or epistemic values, which are shown in the three rightmost columns of the table. Each of these has standards or norms about the extent to which these values can and ought to be realized. The first two rows display the parallel terms in statistics-oriented research and the underlying questions for ethnography. Next are the challenges that frustrate researchers who attempt to realize these objectives. These obstacles are linked to tactics that help, albeit imperfectly, to overcome the challenges.[24]

Table 2.1 Expectations for Ethnographic Method: Criteria, Challenges, and Tactics

Epistemic Value	Veracity	Objectivity	Perspicacity
Conventional equivalent	validity (excluding external validity)	reliability (excluding consistency)	generalizability, external validity
Underlying question	verisimilitude of depiction	transcendence of perspectives	applicability of insights elsewhere
Research process challenges	limits to learning arising in conditions in the field (e.g., danger); limits to learning caused by researcher's personal and role constraints	sensitivity of results to context; risk of reactivity; lack of fully specifiable research context; unknown context-research outcome linkages	inability of method to create insights; hampering of knowledge about where else an insight can "travel" by invalid taxonomies and other challenges of cross-cultural comparison
Related research coping tactics[a]	1. **Prolonged field-work** 2. **Search for disconfirming observations** 3. **Good participative role relationships** 4. **Attentiveness to context** 5. Multiple modes of data collection	1. **Trail of ethnographer's path** 2. Respondent validation 3. Feedback from outsiders 4. (Interrater checks on indexing and coding) 5. (Comprehensive data archive)	1. **Intense consideration of the data** 2. **Exploration**

a. Tactics shown in boldface type are very helpful; those shown in parentheses are of questionable use.

3. WORKING TOWARD VERACITY

Veracity as the First Goal to Target

Trade-offs. With the use of any one research method, or any research instrument, not all goals can be met equally (LeVine, 1981). Consequently, Weick (1979) has advised that researchers ought to "identify the inevitable tradeoffs in inquiry and relax gracefully having done so" (p. 35). Whether or not they can be graceful or relaxed, they can resist trying to maximally realize all possible goals.[25] Ethnographers who adopt the use of conventional research criteria typically prioritize validity. Some, such as Adler and Adler (1995), do hold reliability to be equally applicable, but most would be loath to give away validity in the understandings that they obtain from personal engagements in favor of gains in reliability or generalizability.[26] It appears to follow that veracity takes priority over objectivity and perspicacity. Certainly, the unique terms proposed as ethnographic standards—*apparency, verisimilitude, plausibility, credibility,* and *authenticity*—have much less to do with objectivity or perspicacity than they have to do with veracity.

Veracity has a more mundane orientation to truth than does perspicacity. In Chapter 2, I noted the dictionary definition of *veracity* as devotion to and conformity with truth. For present purposes, this meaning refers to descriptive, or Boasian, truth. *Perspicacity,* by contrast, refers to structuralist, structural functionalist, critical realist, and any other forays toward truth that refer to nonobvious, analytically uncovered understandings. *Perspicacity* refers to veracity that transcends mere description.

How, then, does veracity relate to other research goals, to the goals of "objectivity" and "perspicacity"? In ethnography, as in any study, limitations in satisfying these three epistemic values are limitations in the worth of whatever intimations of truth may be learned. To the extent that objectivity is not achieved, findings are true only from particular persons' perspectives. To the extent that perspicacity is not achieved, findings are (at best) true only in idiosyncratic settings, or (worse) there is no way to know where else, when else, or under what conditions, they could be applied. However, the transcendence of perspectives lacking in veracity, or the transference of insights lacking in veracity, is futile. Without a devotion to descriptive truth, and some success in finding it, all other assertions ring hollow (Lofland, 1995; Maxwell, 1992; see generally Wolcott, 1994).

informants" that signals we "are learning properly" to understand that culture (p. 194). Simply put, it takes time for the inquirer *to undergo* what ethnography is: a process of learning.

Revisits. More time also brings more opportunities to learn the limitations in the researcher's participative role. Roles evolve as the researcher works to develop better empathic links with more and more types of actors (Muecke, 1994). However, correcting for problems in roles may be difficult, and may require disengaging from and revisiting the field "on a new footing" (Foster et al., 1979, p. 331). Although revisits are rare (Stocking, 1992, chap. 7), they are commonly recommended for the study of continuity and change.[33] They also present opportunities for role adjustments and, of course, more time in the field.

Revisits also offer opportunities to seek out acutely reorienting or disconfirming observations, particularly if there has been an effort to anticipate the outcomes that would be predicted by the understanding previously achieved.[34] If this understanding has been published, revisits also offer opportunities for a dialogic form of respondent validation, in which actors respond either to the writings themselves or to their stereotypical image in the site.[35] Although this dialogue can be discomfiting, the only methodological drawback to the postpublication revisit is that the ethnographer's awareness of a possible revisit may constrain the writing, so that it conforms to the actors' norms and values (compare Ellis, 1995).[36]

TACTIC 2: SEEKING OUT REORIENTING
OR DISCONFIRMING OBSERVATIONS

Prolonged fieldwork is a tactic that helps in implementing the generic ethnographic strategy of doggedness and persistence. It establishes a context that enables a patient process of learning. It is not a tactic *of* inquiry itself, but rather a tactic *for* inquiry. The next tactic to be covered, the search for reorienting or disconfirming observations, is a constituent part of ethnographic inquiry. This search is enabled by longer periods of fieldwork, because they increase variation both in what could be observed and in the capacities to notice (Ottenberg, 1994).

Ethnographers consider an observation that does not fit a generalization as invaluable. They consider a sweeping generalization such as *The Kaguru: A Matrilineal People* . . . (the title of Beidelman, 1971) as a challenge to look for exceptions (such as patrilineal properties described on pages 49 and 72). Perhaps, as a generalization, Beidelman's title is defensible, but all generalizations are treated as suspect, all assertions as probationary (Frayser, 1996). Ethnographers seek to revise and reformulate their assertions until they can account for all their observations (Kidder, 1981). To this end, they actively seek out instances that disconfirm or reconfigure the "predictions or expectations" that follow from their explanations (Campbell, 1975, p. 181).[37] To do this, they need data that are rich in both observations and implications.[38] They also need clarity about the expectations that derive from their explanations, without which they could not distinguish aberrant from consistent observations (Fredericks & Miller, 1997).

Few tactics are more fundamental in ethnography, and few are more hidden, more tacit, in published reports. The norm has been (Leach, 1961, p. 21) that good ethnographies reveal enough potential embarrassments to the author's story line that astute readers could catch them on their own (as Gough [1971] did for Evans-Pritchard's account of Nuer kinship). Just how the original ethnographers tracked down any such observations in their own analyses is left to the readers' imaginations. However, as Agar (1991) observes, ethnographic data management software has the capacity to search out any data segment that might call for disconfirmation or reorientation of provisional explanations. In the discussion of data consideration in Chapter 5, I will propose that the outline of this process should be documented within the method discussion.

TACTIC 3: GOOD PARTICIPATIVE ROLE RELATIONSHIPS

Insiders, outsiders, and their interactions. Ethnographers learn (we have seen) about the potential of roles that they play in the field. The ethnographer's approach to learning in general depends on well-crafted participative role relationships. All ethnographic learning is a joint production of the perspective of outsiders (what once was called the etic perspective), the perspective of insiders (the emic perspective), and the interaction between these perspectives.[39] Thus, there are three main questions to ask of these role relationships: What is the extent and nature of the outsider's involvement in insiders' activities? What is the extent and nature of insiders' participation in research? And finally, What is the division of labor, between the outsiders and insiders, within the research process?

In Adler and Adler's (1987) typology, the outsider's involvement ranges from the Peripheral Member Researcher (PMR), through Active Member Researcher (AMR), to Complete Member Researcher (CMR). AMRs, unlike PMRs, are "coparticipants in a joint endeavor" who share insiders' goals, at least in the short term (Adler & Adler, 1987, p. 50). CMRs, by comparison, have "gone native" or converted to insider roles. So long as outsiders, in their personal trajectories, remain fundamentally researchers, they are to that extent not true CMRs (Rabinow, 1977, p. 79).

The typical range of the insider's participation in research ranges from the marginally involved (for example, the trickster fooling the ethnographer) to the key informant and the critic (Emerson & Pollner, 1988). Less typically, at one extreme, the insider is the passive object of observations;[40] at the other extreme, the colleague or even the principal investigator (Learned & Stewart, 1994). In the last case, where the insider is, in some fashion, also an outsider, the researcher has become an auto-ethnographer (Hayano, 1979) conducting "opportunistic" research (Riemer, 1977).

The management of the division of labor between outsiders and insiders is, in part, a question of rhetoric rather than method, in that authors can compose ethnographies in a mode that foregrounds or backgrounds these concerns. "Jointly told tales" (Van Maanen, 1988, pp. 136-138), for example, explicitly recognize a collaborative relationship. The research division of labor is, however, also a question of method. Collaborative, "insider/outsider research teams" (Louis & Bartunek, 1992) are flanked as possibilities, on one hand, by the more or less complete domination of research design and practice by outside professionals who retain full responsibility for research, and on the other hand by the more or less complete domination by insiders.[41]

Role relationships are complex enough to merit treatment in books of their own (e.g., Adler & Adler, 1987). I will simplify this topic two ways. First, I will focus on the outsider's roles, even though ethnographic learning also depends on both the insiders' roles and the insider-outsider relationship. For example, it may be possible to compensate for deficiencies in the outsider's roles, such as a narrow range of contacts, by means of collaboration with insiders, such as those with wide-ranging contacts. Second, as the topic of this book is method, I will consider roles only in terms of their impact on methodological goals.

The outsider's roles affect the capacity to succeed in tactics for improving objectivity (the ethnographer's path; see Chapter 4), veracity (revisits, discussed above), and perspicacity (site selection, within-site sampling, and multiple-site studies; see Chapter 5). They also have a crucial impact on the achievement of veracity. For this goal, artfully crafted role relationships can have important, positive effects. They can generate opportunities for inquiry. They can provide exposure to interactions and performances, in a wide variety of naturalistic, backstage, social contexts. They can also provide access to a wide variety of actors.

Generating opportunities for inquiry. Opportunities for inquiry are enhanced by the outsider's participation as if an insider, at least as an Active Member Researcher, if not as a Complete Member Researcher. Participation in naturalistic roles may be a prerequisite of structural access to a site (Adler & Adler, 1987, pp. 52-53). Even in cases where access might be permitted to passive observers, such roles "are rather unnatural or at least unusual in most settings" (Van Maanen, 1991, p. 31; see also Buchanan, Boddy, & McCalman, 1988). For this reason, observers are drawn into more active involvement (Barley, 1990). Involvement is more natural, and also less intrusive. As Katz (1983) argues, if members react to the outsider as a researcher (or other stranger), the threat of reactivity is greater than if members react to the researcher as if he or she were another member. (Kapferer's [1972, pp. xxi-xxii] experience was one exception; presumably there are others.)

Active participation promotes learning, but not all AMR or CMR roles do this equally. For example, roles offer varying amounts of time for note taking, roaming about, observing, listening, and questioning (Whyte, 1984, p. 29). Roles also offer varying opportunities to learn the insider's role. A very attractive characteristic of an ethnographic role, Coy (1989) has written, is that it "will be the target of other people's attempts to socialize and educate him [with] as little impact as possible on the social system" (p. 117). All ethnographic roles have some of these apprenticelike features, assuming that, as often happens, insiders attempt to train the researcher to behave in ways that are more normatively acceptable, or even, as they see it, more human (Kondo, 1990, p. 16). Formal trainee or apprentice roles, such as those employed by Cooper (1989), Coy (1989), Dalton (1959), and Stewart (1989), make this enculturation function explicit.

Experiencing performance; witnessing performance. Apprentice roles are modes of legitimate peripheral participation (Lave & Wenger, 1991) that enable the novice to learn in interaction with elders and other masters of a community of practice (Coy, 1989; Stoller, 1994). The tacit knowledge that the novice acquires is, according to some anthropologists, much more central to insider culture than is knowledge that can be transmitted explicitly.[42] A recent set of articles by Barth (1989), Bloch (1991), Jenkins (1994), Keesing (1987), Stoller (1994), and Wikan (1991) proposes, in opposition to structuralists and interpretive anthropologists such as Geertz

(1976), that culture is not a detached system of objects to be cognitively "read." Rather, as Barth (1989) proposes, culture is distributed differentially across actors, each of whom confers meaning on signs and symbols based on "her/his particular constellation of experience, knowledge, and orientations" (p. 134).

These anthropological theories have the implication for ethnographic roles that it is not sufficient to interview actors to understand their culture. As Fabian (1991) expresses this, culture is not so much "informative" as it is "performative" (p. 397). Thus, the ethnographer not only needs to have opportunities to witness a variety of performances, but, more fundamentally, needs to experience culture personally (Wikan, 1991). Moreover, because culture is not homogeneous, but is distributed across diverse social contexts, the ethnographer needs experience in multiple contexts.

Skills required. Another implication of the need for experience is the need for any skills that are the prerequisites of participation. The most obvious of these is the need to know the local language (Whyte, 1984, p. 47). For specialized role involvements, knowledge of the specialized idioms and restricted codes used by members of certain professions and crafts, such as software designers, may also be needed (Learned, 1995). Generally, ethnographers may need performance-related skills that are used in occupations, crafts, and professions, and that enable the desired participation.

Providing exposure to interactions and performances. The ethnographer's roles offer varying possibilities for resocialization, and also for opportunities to witness a variety of interactions and performances. Organized social life, comprising families, firms, communities, professions, and so on, presents an artful front to outsiders. Therefore, the involvement of at least the Active Member Researcher is usually needed for witnessing everyday, backstage, and private interactions.[43] Consequently, the researcher obviously ought to report on his or her roles as they affect the range of life observed (Cooper, 1989, p. 146). Less obvious is the need to report not only on the apparently research-related roles that affect social access, but also the apparently private roles, such as friendship, that may also affect research (Obligacion, 1994). For example, Gartrell (1979) learned that the findings of an ethnographer who had previously worked in her field site had been colored by insiders' reactions to his choice of a place in which to live: Unbeknown to the researcher, his housemate was a notorious witch.

Providing access to actors. Varying ethnographer's roles, then, offer varying opportunities to witness a variety of actors and insider roles.[44] Not all field sites involve member beliefs in witches, but virtually all sites have a range of insider cliques and statuses, such that no individual could participate in every one of them (Altheide & Johnson, 1994). Therefore, ethnographers try at the least not to take on roles that foreclose observation of those in which they are not themselves involved. They also try to interact with, and even collaborate with, actors who themselves have a wide range of contacts and sources of knowledge. This requires conscious effort, because "the role assignments allocated" to the researcher by luck and by insiders will, as Coy (1989) observes, often "be quite biased. . . . Field researchers are often first befriended by local immigrants, outcasts, socio-logical orphans, deviants, or adolescents" (p. 116).

TACTIC 4: ATTENTIVENESS TO SPEECH AND INTERACTIONAL CONTEXTS

Notes on speech-in-action. Even should the ethnographer manage to determine which insiders are the best informants, these people may be, by virtue of their ability to bridge the insider and outsider worlds, "marginal" (Rabinow, 1977, p. 39; see also Hammersley, 1990, p. 83). Granted, the capacity to bridge is also an entrepreneurial quality (Stewart & Krackhardt, 1997). However, the most highly "native" of the "natives," the most highly expert of the experts in a culture, are not representative of that culture. Their ideas are *"extrapolations from* [a] cultural tradition, not its quintes-sential expression" (Keesing, 1987, p. 164; see also Dow's commentary in Aunger, 1995). More generally, as Bloch (1991) cautions, "we should treat all explicit knowledge as . . . probably remote from that employed in practical activities under normal circumstances" (p. 194). This is one reason that even the best-intentioned informants find it hard to articulate what it is that people do (Rudie, 1994); that "what people say they do and what they do is so different" (C. Wright Mills, cited by Bernard, 1994, p. 173).

The implication for ethnographers is spelled out by Wolcott (1992): Unless one is satisfied with accounts of only how insiders "believe things *should* be," it is important that one "observe firsthand" instead (pp. 20-21). There is widespread agreement among ethnographers that good method includes the observation and recording not only of interviews, but, more important, of "speech-in-action" (Sanjek, 1990b, p. 211).[45] Key informant interviews are attractively convenient, and are useful for many purposes

(Kleinman, Stenross, & McMahon, 1994). Nevertheless, as Smith (1990) admonishes, ethnographers should "listen carefully to what people say, watch what they do, and keep [their] voices down" (p. 369). Smith's directive to watch what people *do* offers a useful qualification to the preoccupation in the literature, my own discussion here included, with the observation of speech acts.

Contexts of informant speech. Ethnography is a joint construction of understanding between the researcher and the actors (Dreher, 1994; Whyte, 1984, pp. 74, 223). This joint, inquiring relationship is so central to the ethnographic process that its major characteristics must be specified (Emerson, 1987). One of these characteristics has been covered: the capacities in which one inquires (i.e., participative roles). A second will be discussed shortly: the network of actors one engages (i.e., the ethnographer's path). Becker and Geer (1960) also note that the social contexts in which this interaction takes place must be distinguished, with particular attention paid to those most crucial of the actors; those who engage in inquiry at length; those who are called, in the jargon, the informants.

The social context serves to bias—that is, to enable and to constrain— what people say. For example, employees say different things in the presence of peers, supervisors, and ethnographers. From this context-specificity of speech, Becker and Geer (1960) derive two methodological inferences. First, multiple contextual biases should be sampled, naturalistically, as components of the subject matter. Even the bias that is researcher induced can be used to elicit preexisting thoughts and feelings that otherwise could not be articulated.

The second inference Becker and Geer derive is that the contextual biases should be specified. Did the researcher personally draw out an actor's utterance, or was it volunteered? If the latter, was it offered spontaneously to other insiders—was it speech-in-action? Did other actors inhibit what was said, or did they, as they can in focus groups, elicit ideas that would otherwise have remained unarticulated (Morgan, 1988)? Documenting the answers to these sorts of questions, for all of the recorded utterances, would overflow the borders of the method discussion. The ethnographic depiction itself is the place for the researcher to demonstrate sensitivity to the context for utterances and, for that matter, to the context for all other activities and interactions (Birdwhistell, 1970).

Statistics-oriented interview methods. There is an exception, where de- tails of the interview context should be addressed in the method discussion.

Not uncommonly, ethnographers use statistics-oriented techniques, most often censuses or surveys of local social units. Occasionally, ethnographers will code existing studies, create psychometric scales, use interrater agreement checks (see below), or administer structured interviews, in the interest of being able to use reliability tests and other statistical analyses. In these cases, conventional documentation is appropriate (Johnson, 1987). Note, however, that—contrary to Aunger's (1994, 1995) claims—these exceptions apply only to the ethnographic use of *nonethnographic* method tactics.[46] Moreover, the purpose of this documentation is the pursuit not of veracity but of objectivity.

TACTIC 5: MULTIPLE MODES
OF DATA COLLECTION

Aunger has successfully demonstrated the value of nonethnographic interviewing in ethnographic projects. Although observing speech-in-action may be more ethnographic than interviewing, for some purposes interviews are more fruitful (Kleinman et al., 1994). For example, one likely needs to witness to uncover political manipulations of kinship (e.g., Gulliver, 1971; Turner, 1957; Van Velsen, 1964), but to delineate genealogies, direct solicitation is typically necessary. Moreover, long interviews (McCracken, 1988) and focus groups (Morgan, 1988) offer opportunities for insiders to think and express ideas about topics that get neglected or suppressed in ordinary, spontaneous conversations.[47]

Interview and participant observation data are two modes that are appropriate in ethnography. Other modes include data from documents produced by insiders, documents produced by outsiders, physical artifacts, surveys, and nonparticipative observation. In all forms of qualitative research, just as in other research, the use of multiple modes of data collection—or triangulation—is an important tactic in the service of veracity.[48]

Triangulation is important because no one type of data, and no one particular informant, is error-free (Shulman, 1994). LeVine (1981) holds that "like other scientists (and other animals) the ethnographer struggles for knowledge with fallible instruments for knowing. His distinctive sources of information come equipped with distinctive biases, and his task is to design data collection strategies for superseding these biases, usually by finding additional sources with different biases" (p. 180). As LeVine implies, the use of multiple sources is not a mechanical technique, but is rather "an active attempt [by the inquirer] to refute a [provisional] generalization" in the search for disconfirming data (Elsworth, 1994, p. 335).

Only the researcher who has pursued this route can present, in the report, the "massive over-determination of pattern" (Agar, 1996, pp. 37, 40-41) that testifies—more eloquently than the method section itself—to the quality of the effort to achieve veracity.

Tactics summary. Some accomplishment in the effort to achieve veracity is a precondition for the other research goals. Some accomplishment in the major method tactics that promote veracity is a precondition of a good ethnography. Such an ethnography is impossible without sufficient time in the field, diligence in seeking out reorienting or disconfirming observations, participant observer roles that offer broad access to insider life, and attentiveness to the context in which speech and other acts are observed. Such an ethnography is achievable, perhaps, but certainly limited, without a variety of sources of data.

4. WORKING TOWARD OBJECTIVITY

Objectivity as a Goal

Reliability. Statistics-oriented researchers bundle both *objectivity* and *consistency* into the research goal "reliability." This makes sense for them, because objectivity (in the sense of the relative independence of results from particularities of the researcher) and consistency (the independence of results from time of observation) are both instances of the independence of results from the research circumstances. This bundling does not, however, make sense for ethnographers, whose research is inherently embedded in complex, longer-term social contexts. One implication that could be derived is that reliability is not an appropriate goal for ethnographers. This implication is popular. For most ethnographers, "issues of reliability have received"—and warrant—"little attention" (Kirk & Miller, 1986, p. 42). For Sanjek (1990a), concern for ethnographic " 'reliability' verges on affectation" (p. 394). For Wolcott (1994, p. 159), efforts to achieve it would strip away the value of participant observation.

But this is not a satisfactory conclusion for those ethnographers (such as Aunger, 1994, 1995; Kidder, 1981) who do not choose to waive their right to make an effort at reliability. If ethnographers are to make this effort, they need to draw a different implication from that of Sanjek and Wolcott from the complex circumstances of their research. That alternative implication is the need to recognize that reliability is a multidimensional construct. Objectivity ought first to be unbundled from consistency, which, as I have argued in Chapter 2, is a misdirected value for ethnographers.

Next, the dimensions or subconcepts of objectivity ought to be distinguished. After objectivity is unbundled into its dimensions, it becomes apparent that these dimensions differ both in their potential realization in ethnography and in their repertoires of helpful method tactics. Reliability, *qua* objectivity, is a concept that refers to three distinct dimensions or subconstructs: bias (the effect of researcher or interactional peculiarities on results), replication (the reproduction of identical results by other researchers), and specification (the definition of research circumstances, so that bias can be judged and replication can be attempted). In ethnography, there are potent tactics that mitigate bias. There are tactics that help in specifying—albeit incompletely—the research circumstances. There are, however, no humanly possible tactics that enable replication.

Bias. Ethnography is affected, to a greater or lesser extent, by the personal characteristics and orientations of researchers and of insider informants (Lofland & Lofland, 1995, pp. 74-75). It is also affected by the interpersonal dynamics and interactions between researchers and insiders (Gartrell, 1979). Reviewers of an ethnography can therefore ask, To what extent, and in what ways, were the results affected by the peculiarities of researchers, insiders, or their interactions? How well were their biases, and the reactivity of insiders to researchers, minimized or offset by the use of research method? To what extent can we answer these questions?

Specification. This last question addresses not only bias but also specification. Reviewers could ask two questions regarding this dimension of objectivity. The first is, Has the research basis—including the data—been specified sufficiently that readers could make their own informed judgments about the interpretation and findings that are presented? The second question really ought not to be asked: Has the research procedure been specified sufficiently that the study could be replicated? The problem with this question is the expectation that an ethnography can be replicated, in the same sense as a laboratory experiment. Thornton (1988) adds that ethnographic thinking includes the writing, which, like the fieldwork, "cannot be replicated" (p. 292). None of the research method tactics that I recommend in this book are designed in aid of replication. A less quixotic question, and a useful one, to be covered in Chapter 5, is, Have the context and results been sufficiently specified that the findings could potentially be disconfirmed in a follow-up study? [49] Replicability is not a precondition for scientific findings; intersubjective testability is (Hunt, 1991, p. 51; see also Hunt, 1994; Kirk & Miller, 1986).

Inevitable Limits on Objectivity

Sensitivity of results to contexts. Geertz (1988) contends that "the highly situated nature of ethnographic description—this ethnographer, in this time, in this place, with these informants, and these experiences" makes of his or her work *necessarily* "the imagined [but not] the imaginary, the fictional [but not] the false" (pp. 5, 140). In the next chapter, I will question the ideographic rhetoric of Geertz's conclusion. However, Geertz's account of the subject is a felicitous introduction to the topic at hand, the limits to objectivity.

As Geertz argues, ethnographic understanding is deeply "situated," and by my count it is so three times over. First, it is situated in Geertz's sense, by the specificities of time, place, and persons in the research process. This sense is that invoked by Sanjek's (1990a) concept of "the ethnographer's path," documentation of which is the first of the objectivity-enhancing tactics discussed below. Second, ethnographic understanding is situated by the myriad historical, local minutiae that may be needed to interpret the "native's point of view" (Geertz, 1976). For example, ritual objects, symbols of identity, and speech acts recurrently change in meaning with changes in the setting, thus rendering them unintelligible when abstracted from their context.[50] Third, ethnographic understanding is situated in holistic explanations, referencing cultural and social systems. For example, a particular pattern of kinship will be explained by reference to a context that includes, say, some combination of religious, political, economic, and ecological considerations.[51]

Ethnographic inquiry is highly situated. Further, it *situates itself* in the research setting. Because of participant observation, it raises the risk of reactivity, of impacts of the process of research on the field setting itself. Some degree of reactivity is inevitable. For example, ethnographic interviews (for that matter, all interviews) are confounded by interviewer, interactional, and situational differences (Aunger, 1994; Obligacion, 1994). As Hammersley (1990) puts it, the critical question about reactivity "is whether or not the research process or the characteristics of the researcher have affected the behavior that was observed . . . in respects that are relevant to the claims made (and to a significant degree)" (p. 81). Gittelsohn, Shankar, West, Ram, and Gnywali (1997) measured the impact of observation in a field setting and found "the level of reactivity [to be] low" (p. 188) and also (as others had found before them) that it declines very rapidly over the period of observations.

Agar (1986b, p. 36) is right, it appears, in arguing that the outsider's impact on the insiders is very easy to "overrate," as ethnographers tend to be minor players in practical life. They are legitimate *peripheral* participants (Lave & Wenger, 1991). However, the impact that insiders have on them may well be more significant. The risk in this reverse reactivity is that inquiry becomes fettered, or subtly coerced, due to the ethnographer's sense of obligation and commitment to norms of reciprocity, to "reply in kind" to the hospitality and prestations of frankness from people in power (Firth, 1977, p. 10).[52]

Difficulty of specifying contexts. If the research context affects research results, the solution that appears to follow, and that is often recommended, is to specify that context.[53] That proves to be easier said than done. For example, Aunger (1995) would require that the ethnographer "specify fully the context of the data collection event" (p. 99). As de Ruijter and Duveen both correctly object, in their responses to his prescription, this would be literally impossible (Aunger, 1995, pp. 116, 118). The full context of ethnography is emergent and largely tacit. It is also complex. For example, Heider (1988) lists more than a dozen possible types of differences among ethnographers that might affect their research.[54] Jaarsma and de Wolf (1991) add to the list ethnographers' differences in external ties to patrons, governments, and gatekeepers. Cohen (1992) points out that these differences persist in affecting the research in the "postfieldwork" phase. Therefore, in spite of initial efforts to provide a universal template of all the context information of methodological significance (e.g., Altheide & Johnson, 1994, p. 494), many ethnographers would agree with Fabian (1995, p. 47) that the elements of ethnographic contexts are not universal or "given"; that, on the contrary, each context is actively created by multiple actors. It is very unlikely that there will ever be a determination of the template for the entire research context.

Unknown context-research causation. Let us suppose—or hope—that the argument above is wrong. Let us imagine that a consensus has emerged on all the contextual factors that affect research and that ought, therefore, to be specified. Let us further imagine that this information could, in practice, be documented. Can it now be further imagined that this information could then be adequately interpreted? There are two reasons it could not.

The first reason for skepticism refers to an analogous situation: the difficulties in interpreting other ethnographers' field notes. Understanding another person's field notes is an onerous, time-consuming practice that requires extensive contextual knowledge on the part of the reader (Lutkehaus, 1990; Smith, 1990). Fully disclosed contextual information would not be materially easier to understand. The second reason for skepticism refers to the absence of a comprehensive and validated theory that accounts for contextual effects. Evidently, there is no such theory that can account for the effect of all feasible patterns of interactions. Moreover, there is no such theory that could account even for the effect of the traits of a single researcher. Let us simplify even further and consider only personal, nonprofessional traits. In Heider's (1988) account, the main such traits are gender, age, family status, size, sexual preference, and race. Although these variables are relatively amenable to study, one still cannot claim to know their effects on a comprehensive range of research outcomes.

Research Coping Tactics

TACTIC 1: TRAIL OF THE ETHNOGRAPHER'S PATH

In the interests of objectivity, ethnographers must account for the processes through which they have learned (Malinowski, 1922/1961, pp. 2-3). They can do so by adopting a "reflexive" writing style that incorporates, into the descriptive account, their experience of learning as participant observers. In Wolcott's (1990b) witticism, "The important thing is to be up-front about it, but that is not the same as putting it up front" (p. 27). According to this logic, "autobiography can . . . be a condition of . . . ethnographic objectivity in the sense that it allows the writing subject's actual history and involvement to be considered critically" (Fabian, 1991, p. 382). For example, "narrative ethnographies" (Tedlock, 1991) and "confessional tales . . . attempt to show how a reader might work back from a display of the conditions under which the fieldwork was accomplished to some assessment of" validity and reliability (Van Maanen, 1988, p. 92). These reflexive literary presentations may be necessary to reflect fully the complex, emergent interactions of researchers and insiders. However, it is simpler to document these interactions in the research method discussion.

In this alternative, the writer specifies what Sanjek (1990a, pp. 398-400) calls "the ethnographer's path," meaning the network of informants and contacts that the researcher engages. Sanjek makes the case that knowledge of this network helps in the assessment of a study's validity, for reasons similar to those adduced about participative roles in the previous chapter. Although roles are more relevant for veracity and the path more relevant for objectivity, each of these tactics helps promote both of the goals. The primary question resolved by the choice of participative roles is, *In what capacities does one undergo and observe* interactions and performances? Only indirectly does it answer the question of *whom* one interacts with.[55] Roles provide *potential* for sets of interactions; the ethnographer's path is the set of actual interactions as this potential has been *realized* and the "who" of all the other parties, like names on a dance card, has been entered. Veracity is directly enabled by the multiplicity of these interactions. Objectivity is served, albeit less directly, by the "dance card" itself, which documents the fieldwork component of research, and which provides an accounting for, and hence perhaps serves to keep in check, the biases of the informants and observer.

What should be documented? The dance card is a metaphor, but so too are terms like *network* and *path*. These metaphors fail to answer precisely what does and does not need to be included in the record. Sanjek's (1990a) general description of this tactic implies few limitations on what to include. Besides the "size and range" (p. 400) of the network, Sanjek directs authors to disclose information on all the informants and actors who were observed, including demographic data, such as gender, occupation, and age, and also disclose (apparently) the actual network path of access from one informant to another. Similarly sweeping are the proposals by Muecke (1994, p. 196) and by Werner and Schoepfle (1987, vol. 2, pp. 280, 331). J. C. Johnson (1990) contributes techniques for determining the attribute and network qualities of key informants. The ideal, presumably, would be multimethod social network analyses, at multiple times, that include the ethnographer and all his or her nontrivial contacts, including (to be relentlessly logical) all nontrivial contacts for all key informants.[56]

Another approach to documenting the ethnographer's path, which would provide a great deal of summary information, would be quite feasible with the use of qualitative data software packages such as the Ethnograph (Seidel, Kjolseth, & Seymour, 1988; Tesch, 1990). For each actor, one could report the number of data segments in which that actor is the speaker or is for any other reason tagged (i.e., indexed, or coded). With sufficient effort, one could also calculate the total time spent in each actor's presence. One could then categorize actors by gender, or any other meaningful distinction, to summarize the observations of each of these categories. Admittedly, this approach would fall short of a detailed disclosure, on a moment-by-moment, actor-by-actor basis of the total network path. Such an exhaustive accounting is clearly impractical, and in practice impossible. The only reason even to make the attempt would be to invite a replication, but this documentation of the historical specifics would serve only to demonstrate the absurdity of that objective itself.

Apparently, then, calls for depiction of the ethnographer's path are not to be interpreted literally. It follows that what should, realistically, be presented is not a question of adherence to a checklist or a template to be applied to all ethnographies, but rather a question of standards, of norms about accomplishment. Moreover, the ethnographic literature does provide the basis for some guidelines. Implicit in this literature are five questions that help to judge if an account is up to standards.

The first two questions refer to ethnographic sampling. The first is, Does the account provide basic *information on "informants and contacts. . . those . . . talked to and observed"* (Sanjek, 1990a, p. 399; italics added)? This question raises the prospect that many actors ought to be sampled (Rosen, 1991), and certainly more than a handful ought to be, as no individual represents the range of actor diversity, and any one informant could be undependable (Adler & Adler, 1995; Dow's commentary in Aunger, 1995; Naroll, 1970a; Werner & Schoepfle, 1987, vol. 1, pp. 170-171). However, the purpose of this quantity is qualitative, the objective being to achieve "strategic coverage of the system" (Johnson, 1990, p. 26). The second, and more critical, question about the ethnographer's path is, Does this information shed light on the *range of variation in perspectives* that were witnessed, in what ways, to what degree?

A good ethnography is expected to sample the entire distribution, and not just central tendencies, of the topics studied (Johnson, 1990; Schwartzman, 1993, pp. 53-55). As Werner and Bernard (1994) argue, "What good ethnographic sampling is about [is] establishing the range of phenomena, not establishing the proportions of traits in a population at large" (p. 8). Thus, such sampling is not about selecting actors or inter-actions randomly. Random sampling would promote both objectivity and generalizability (for which reasons Johnson & Johnson, 1990, do recommend its use), but it is quite infeasible, and ill-advised, in most participative contexts. For example, organizational ethnographers who sampled time and place randomly (following Johnson and Johnson's prescriptions) would have a lot of explaining to do to insiders, and would miss most significant performances (Brim & Spain, 1974, pp. 84-86; Buchanan et al., 1988). They would also miss the ultimate purpose of sampling for ethnography, which is to maximize the range of comparisons and opportunities for disconfirmations.

Those informants whose views are reflected without much critique or qualification are expected to be credible (Becker, 1970, chap. 2; Hammersley, 1990, pp. 82-83; Rabinow, 1977, pp. 39, 73, 95). They are expected to be, as Dalton (1967) puts it, "the best-informed informants" (p. 87). However, for the same reasons that the ethnographer's ability is not a topic in method discussions, as a rule the descriptions and interpretations presented are sufficient testimony to the informants' understanding.[57]

The other three questions about the account of the path also strike to the roots of ethnographic quality. First, does this information make possible an assessment of the *extent and type of partisanship* on the part of the author (Becker, 1970, pp. 111, 123, 131; Jaarsma & de Wolf, 1991; Wolcott, 1992)? Second, does this information clarify the researcher's manner of, and success in, *gaining the trust of multiple subgroups* (Gartrell, 1979; Lofland, 1995)? Third, does this information reveal the researcher's success in attaining a *deep and privileged access* within at least some social units? All of these questions can be answered without any reference to method discussions, by the ethnographic depiction itself. Because the assessment of a study is overdetermined, the impossibility of reporting the total path is not the threat to objectivity that it may at first appear.

For this very reason, one could question whether or not the path really needs to be included in the method discussion. There are three reasons in favor of inclusion. The first is the disciplining effect of this, or any other, expectation of an explicit accounting of method on research practice itself. The second is efficiency. Summary information will save many pages of confessional journal space and hours of difficult writing time. The third is discovery. With very complex data sets, it is unlikely that the ethnographer really knows all the answers to the questions listed above.

Take, for example, the final question, on success in gaining deep and privileged access. Referring to the field note record as a gestalt, this question could be answered by summaries of segments of text that have been tagged with codes—"COMPLAINT," "RIVALRY," "BLAME," for example—that demonstrate the researcher's success in getting the backstage scoop. Most researchers, one suspects, would have a pretty good feel for their overall success in this regard, and would not be surprised by such summaries. One also suspects that most would find a surprise if they were to cross-tabulate these code words with actor names or categories of actors. For example, it might be that the researcher has succeeded in learning more about the private "HOPES" of one group and about the private "ANXIETIES" of another.[58]

TACTIC 2: RESPONDENT VALIDATION

An interview or focus group, as we have seen in Chapter 3, can offer to the actors a rare chance to reflect upon their lives. So also can requests for feedback on research reports written on their worlds. Whether or not the researcher offers actors the chance to read a preliminary draft or summary, it has become less and less likely that ethnography's "subjects and its audience" are separable (Geertz, 1988, p. 132). As noted above, "when they read what we write" (the title of a recent collection—see Davis, 1993), "they"—the insiders—may reveal a markedly different perspective from that of the writer (see also Ellis, 1995; Mahmood & Armstrong, 1992; Ottenberg, 1990, 1994). Such discrepancies are not, in themselves, wicked, but they do imply a potential for the researcher to explore them explicitly prior to publication.

This potential can be realized in two ways. It would be realized without further ado in research based on insider-outsider collaboration (Louis & Bartunek, 1992). Otherwise, it could be realized by oral or written feedback by insiders on research reports. This tactic, sometimes called *respondent validation,* has been advocated by nonethnographic field researchers (Guba, 1981; Yin, 1984, pp. 137-140).

Ethnographers have been somewhat more equivocal in their endorsements, and inclined to point to limitations in this practice. Their research is inherently based on insider-outsider dialogue, with or without respondent validation, and they are reluctant to accord a privileged epistemological status to more formal means of feedback.[59] In ethnographers' experience, insiders typically lack the desire or the scholarly background to read their reports, with the consequence that the feedback tends to be ambiguous (Silverman, 1993, p. 159). Unless the feedback is very elementary, it is also liable to include errors of its own. Ultimately, the responsibility for description and for interpretation must rest with the writer (Emerson & Pollner, 1988; Hammersley, 1990, p. 83). Further, unless ethnographers study in remote and little-known cultures, a major "warrant" for research is their ability to learn what insiders do not themselves recognize (Katz, 1997; see also Dauber, 1995). Ethnographers are, moreover, reluctant to risk attempts by powerful insiders to veto publication (Whyte, 1984, p. 196; Wolcott, 1990b, p. 45).

Despite these limitations, respondent validation may have some value. At the least, it can supply new data that include potential for insight into the researcher-actor relationship (Emerson & Pollner, 1988). It could also help maintain that relationship, because it may be an expected form of "professional courtesy" (Yin, 1984, p. 138). In statistics-oriented language, it can help to improve a study's "construct validity" (Yin, 1984, p. 139) and "accuracy" (Buchanan et al., 1988, p. 63). Further, its incorporation into the research of opinions and judgments, distinct from those of the ethnographer, enhances objectivity. Like feedback from outsiders, which is the next tactic to be covered, respondent validation increases the range of subjectivities represented, and may decrease any inclinations of the researcher to use the inquiry as the projection of personal bias.

TACTIC 3: FEEDBACK FROM OUTSIDERS

Team-based ethnographic projects offer advantages in access to multiple perspectives from multiple social positions (Foster et al., 1979; Louis & Bartunek, 1992). Teams thereby promote objectivity in two ways: They diversify the ethnographer's path (and participative roles), and they provide each researcher a source of feedback from another scholar. Team-based ethnographies are launched most typically on the basis of student-adviser or conjugal relationships. However, outside the field of rapid, applied research, their use has been sporadic. Their rarity may be due more to academic tradition than to any method drawbacks. There is, admittedly, one principal drawback. Teams are likely to hinder objectivity by increasing reactivity. Compared with solo researchers, teams are more intrusive and disruptive in almost any setting (Stocking, 1992, p. 39).

Another, even rarer, mode of access to multiple perspectives is the use of multiple interviewers (Aunger, 1994, employed multiple interviewers— not for this purpose, but for reliability tests). A much more widespread way for the field-worker to access multiple perspectives is through informal feedback from other researchers (Guba, 1981; Rosenblatt, 1981). Although it would be helpful if these others could be "knowledgeable about the setting" (Wolcott, 1994, p. 349), their only necessary quality is a willingness to engage the ethnographer in depth. Such an opportunity for critique can be reason enough for a researcher to interrupt time in the field for a visit home (Foster et al., 1979; Whyte, 1984, p. 27).

Outsider feedback from other scholars is ubiquitous. However, if it is documented at all, it is consigned to notes of acknowledgment, not the method discussion. The way to include it in the latter would be to treat significant linkages with other researchers as arcs in the ethnographer's path (Jaarsma & de Wolf, 1991).[60]

TACTIC 4: INTERRATER CHECKS ON INDEXING AND CODING

The use of code words figures prominently in my discussion in Chapter 5 of ethnographic analysis or data consideration. If that emphasis is well-founded, surely there ought to be interrater checks on bias in coding. Silverman (1993, pp. 148-149) has advocated this use of a statistics-oriented tactic in qualitative research. So too have Miles and Huberman (1994), who propose a goal of 80% to 90% "intra- and intercoder agreement" (p. 64).[61] Based on my years of Active Member Research in business schools, I suspect that this calculation is a methodological fetish that reviewers will expect. Unfortunately, it will be argued, it is just that, a fetish, providing spurious protection. Before this argument can be made, the meaning of *coding* in this context must be clarified, because coding in ethnography is not the same as coding in conventional (i.e., statistical) research. Fortunately, Becker, Gordon, and LeBailly (1984) have contributed to such a clarification.[62]

Conventional "coding" and ethnographic "indexing." Ethnographic and conventional coding differ on four dimensions. One of these dimensions consists of the logical relationships among code categories. Conventional code categories are mutually exclusive. For example, if an actor is categorized within one age range, no other ranges can also apply. Ethnographic categories could similarly be mutually exclusive, but there is no expectation that they need to be (Becker et al., 1984). Not that ethnographers think that an individual actor can at the same time be 22 and 73 years old—still, an individual actor could be 73 while discussing the time when he or she was 22. An individual actor could simultaneously feel grateful and resentful, loyal and disloyal. Additionally, a single segment of text could be coded for multiple actors; say, one of them 22 years old and the other 73. Because of the next dimension of difference to be noted, this is illogical in conventional coding, but not in ethnography.

A second dimension of difference is the transparency of the units of coded data. In statistics-oriented research, after a unit of data has been coded, from the perspective of its visibility to the researcher, it disappears into an algorithm. In ethnography, it literally reappears, cycle after cycle, each time notes are reread or one of its codes is invoked in retrieval. Conventional data units are opaque; ethnographic data units are transparent. Because the former are impenetrable objects of mathematical manipulation, they must also be fixed, specified, and equivalent; by contrast, the latter can be open, unspecified, and nonequivalent (Becker et al., 1984, p. 21). For these reasons, the ethnographer is free, indeed encouraged, to code promiscuously; "that is, any incident should be coded under a category if there is any reason to believe that it might be considered relevant" (Becker & Geer, 1960, p. 281; see also Emerson et al., 1995, pp. 150-155).

A third dimension of difference is the procedure for assigning codes to data. Conventional coding requires that the rules for doing this are strictly defined in advance. In ethnography, it may be possible to document the connections between codes and data after the fact. However, the process by which they are discerned, or "noticed" (Seidel et al., 1988, chap. 7), is both emergent and provisional (Miles & Huberman, 1994, p. 58; Sanjek, 1990a; Seidel et al., 1988, p. 8-1; Tesch, 1990, p. 253).

A fourth dimension of difference is flagged by Seidel and Kelle (1995). The referent of a conventional code is a variable aspect of a phenomenon; the referent is a "fact." Ethnographers can use codes with this meaning. They too may notice the sorts of variables that are used in conventional coding. If they then tag, or attach, a code word such as *male* to a segment of their data, they need not necessarily ask any more questions about "maleness." They may take as a given that the actors tagged as male are male. If they do this, the term *male* will function as a "code," just as it does in conventional research. However, in ethnography it need not function this way. Researchers could use the word as an "index," in which event the referent is not a fact, but a segment of text to be retrieved and queried again. If they do this, the term *male* will function instead as an index. In Seidel and Kelle's (1995) terminology, a "code" serves a "factual" function, whereas an "index" serves a "referential" function (pp. 58-59). Because the latter is more typical in ethnography, I will henceforth typically use the term *index word* instead of the potentially misleading and conventionally slanted term *code*.

Discounting interrater consensus. Intended as a measure of objectivity, interrater agreement measures only the similarity of similar raters. That is, it is a very modest indicator of intersubjectivity. It has been found empirically to measure cultural homogeneity (Naroll, 1970a), familiarity with a phenomenon (Rothstein, 1990), and socialization into a scholarly subculture (Hak & Bernts, 1996). This problem is compounded when the object of intended agreement is the meaning of ethnographic field notes, which are notoriously difficult to interpret without deep understanding of both the theoretical and sociocultural contexts (Agar, 1991; Jackson, 1990; Kirk & Miller, 1986, pp. 54-55; Lutkehaus, 1990; Silverman, 1993, p. 69; Smith, 1990). As Seidel et al. (1988) warn, you may have to " 'teach' [others] how to 'see' the data as you have come to see it" (p. 7-8). If one does teach others to do this, by Rescher's (1997) stringent standards, one has achieved only cliquish or "parochial subjectivity" (p. 4). One has achieved a complaisant interrater statistic[63] but ought to be charged with misleading advertising if this achievement is brandished as a token of objectivity.

One reason that this claim would be deceptive has already been suggested. That is, the interrater statistic is a faithful indicator of how well the ethnographer has trained the other rater. However, it is an unreliable indicator of intersubjectivity in the wider, educated public. A second reason is that high levels of interrater agreement cannot be achieved, with well-indexed data, if more than one person performs the task of open or first-order indexing. This type of indexing, unlike conventional coding, is open-ended (the third difference noted above). Therefore, the more comprehensive and intensive this indexing—the more the interests of veracity are served—the lower the likelihood that the second indexer would tag with precisely the same words. This provokes a contradiction between veracity and objectivity, which suggests a contradiction between validity and reliability.

Surely there must be a resolution to this paradox. On inspection, this paradox is simply more acute in ethnography than it is in conventional research. In the latter also, the more difficult the rating task, the more the need for training of the raters, and the less the raters represent the wider population (Rothstein, 1990). Moreover, these raters do not create the coding scheme itself anymore than they do, as *raters,* in ethnography. In both cases, the secondary raters are effectively restricted to agreeing or disagreeing with the efforts of the scholars who developed the coding or indexing systems. In both cases, secondary raters provide a check on Type I, but not on Type II, errors. (This distinction has been applied to ethnographic and qualitative research by Kirk & Miller, 1986, pp. 29-30; Silverman, 1993, p. 149.)[64] Type I errors would cause injury with coding-based analysis, where the "facts" and the coded data vanish into equations. When the "coding" is actually indexing (that is, referential), Type I errors are much less wounding, "since the data [after they have been indexed and retrieved] will be subject to further inspection and human judgement" (Becker et al., 1984, p. 22). The data and their indexing remain transparent.

Thus, Type I errors in ethnography amount more to insult than to injury, as there will be many opportunities for reconsideration in the cycles of considering the data. Further, the use of raters to check on Type I errors would only generate an interrater agreement statistic of suspect value as a measure of the level of objectivity. With both these reservations, checks for Type I errors can still be worth the effort. These checks offer a form of outsider feedback, and, like that tactic, they testify to objectivity in two senses, both less stringent than Rescher's. Claims are objective to the extent that they are intersubjective: They are not merely personal judgments, and they can be subjected to disconfirmation, or reinforcement, by other researchers. Moreover, checks of the indexing can help to clarify and refine the indexing system, and, every now and then, they will expose a Type I error. They could also be used to help correct for Type II errors.

In ethnography, Type II errors—the failure to recognize or notice what could be perceived in the data—can be very destructive. Unlike a Type I error, a Type II error may well be a failure in objectivity that also harms the effort to achieve veracity. In order to pursue alternative explanations (Brewer, 1994), researchers need the capacity "to turn up every relevant item of evidence (especially items which might negate [their] propositions)" (Becker et al., 1984, p. 21). An item that is tagged with a misleading or mistaken term (in a Type I error) will be retrieved, and hence it may well be retagged. An item that is mistakenly *not tagged* with a particular term (in a Type II error) cannot be retrieved in searches for that index or code.

Fortunately, there are other ways in which a Type II error may be righted. First, the entire record may be reread; second, untagged items will still be retrieved if they have been tagged with one or more related index terms. This is a justification both for full or saturating indexing and for casting a broad net in index word searches. Two of the tactics that have already been covered, respondent validation and feedback from outsiders, could also help the researcher recover from Type II errors by generating alternative explanations.

A fifth resolution of Type II errors, unlike the first four, corrects directly for missing index terms. In our discussion so far, the second person or inspector has been a "rater" who audits an indexed data record, taking the indexing scheme as a given. However, this other person could instead create his or her own indexing and coding of the data. The effectiveness of this approach in generating previously unexamined interpretations would be improved through maximization of the sociocultural, experiential, and ideological differences between the researcher and the other field note readers.[65]

There is also a sixth way in which Type II (and Type I) errors could be corrected. Interrater checks and efforts at reindexing are intended to check on and correct the indexing and coding. They are not checks of the data themselves (Hinds, Scandrett-Hibdon, & McAulay, 1990). There is another tactic that does promote checking on both the indexing and the data. However, as I explain in the next section, it is a seriously limited tactic: the definitely exacting, and probably preposterous, tactic of a comprehensive data archive.

TACTIC 5: COMPREHENSIVE DATA ARCHIVE

Several qualitative researchers—none of them ethnographers—have claimed that neutrality, replicability, dependability, and other desirable outcomes are served by the creation of data archives for "auditing" by other researchers.[66] Their prescription would require that a *complete, detailed record* be kept "of all methodological decisions made throughout the study" (Rodgers & Cowles, 1993, p. 221; see also Schwandt & Halpern, 1988, p. 79). Ethnographers would be unwise, on both methodological and practical grounds, to follow this advice. Nevertheless, reviewers (and possibly novice ethnographers) might have been influenced by the authors just cited, and there are certain benefits to ethnographic data archives. Therefore, I really ought not do what I would prefer to do, which is quietly to boycott their thesis.

Arguments for audit trails. Three major benefits have been claimed for an auditable trail of the research process. One is enhancement of objectivity by means of increasing the potential for disconfirmability (Hammersley, 1997). This outcome does appear to follow, but an audit trail is not the only means to this end. A second benefit is enhancement of research quality by means of disciplining researchers with the prospect of an audit (Schwandt & Halpern, 1988, p. 25). I have argued in Chapter 2 that the prospect of writing a method discussion is sufficient for this purpose. However, I must admit that neither Schwandt and Halpern (1988) nor this book has any evidence for the purported causal connections. One could argue that method discussions have beneficial outcomes that are assured, such as conforming to many journals' standards. The only outcome of auditable archives that is assured is increased use of paper. However, a third major benefit that can be claimed for this tactic is reduction of scientific fraud (Fox, 1994). It would be satisfying if one could peremptorily dismiss this concern as pointless, but this is unfortunately not possible.

The fraudulent fabrication of data is the most prevalent in fields where money is the motivator, such as biotechnology (Fox, 1994; Goodstein, 1991). However, even my own dear discipline of origin, anthropology, has not been immune, having bestowed upon an incredulous public the celebrated Piltdown forgery (see Tobias, 1994) and the Tasaday fiasco (see Berreman, 1991). After all, dishonesty can be motivated not by money, but by ambitions for professional recognition. It can also be encouraged by the anticipated failures of the editorial review process to detect a well-crafted falsification (Fox, 1994) and (worryingly) by the low likelihood of replication (Goodstein, 1991; Tobias, 1994). Moreover, it is all very well for Lofland and Lofland (1995) to decree that ethnographic reports ought to flag any "possible difficulties and shortcomings in" their data (p. 151). There is no guarantee that ethnographers would recognize what they should report, even if they wished to comply.

Arguments against audit trails. Deception and self-deception are problems, but audits are not the solution. Ethnographers who are bent on fast payback find it easier to race in and out of their fieldwork, do a slipshod job with the literature, and gloss over recalcitrant data than to go to all the bother of inventing field notes, memos, and indexing systems. Why would they go to the trouble of creating counterfeit records when all they need to do in order to slant their documentation is to seize abundant opportunities for selectivity in field note writing and recall? Thus, "in ethnography doctoring data is more difficult to detect than in a [natural] science" (Werner & Schoepfle, 1987, vol. 2, p. 326). There is no guarantee that an audit would detect such doctoring.

One reason an audit would flounder is that another person's field notes, even meticulous field notes, are exceedingly difficult to interpret. This reason has already been identified in the discussions of interpreting context-research linkages and of interrater agreement, and needs no further elaboration. A second reason, however, is a corollary that has not yet been noted. Because of the difficulties of interpreting the record, an audit would be very time-consuming. Schwandt and Halpern (1988, p. 26) estimate that an audit would take 7 to 10 days. Considering their extravagant optimism about the audit process overall—they argue, for example, that it should be "possible for the auditor to 'replay' any portion of the inquiry" (p. 78)—it is unlikely that their estimate of the time requirement is unduly pessimistic.

Most scholars have little enough time to act as reviewers and editors. These latter roles also cause quite enough interpersonal and political tensions within the academy.[67]

A third reason an audit would flounder is that "the research process can never be made fully explicit" (Hammersley, 1997, p. 135). Given its topic of method discussions, this book tends to be an advocate for specification. Therefore, let me be very explicit about explicitness: There is *no possibility at all* that an audit could detect the most fundamental process that results in ethnographic understanding. (Muecke, 1994, is particularly clear on this point.) The auditing metaphor (well, it seems to be a metaphor, but Schwandt & Halpern [1988, p. 74] regard it literally) radically inflates the value of the documented record and radically discounts the value of creativity, theorizing, headnotes or memory, and other elements of "post-fieldwork fieldwork" (Cohen, 1992).[68] Auditors would surely be flummoxed by Leach's *Political Systems of Highland Burma* or Srinivas's *The Remembered Village,* both well-regarded ethnographies that were written after the authors' field notes had been lost or destroyed (Mayer, 1989).

All objectivity-related tactics are limited by the implicit, emergent character of ethnographic learning. However, some tactics, such as the specification of the means by which data are considered and the trail of the ethnographer's path, remain effective with summary documentation. Auditing is impotent with any such compromise. Faced with the herculean task of specifying the tacit process of inquiry, auditors respond by insisting that the ethnographer "compulsively" record each and every method decision, blind alley, intuition, formal analysis, comparison within and beyond the data, and "speculation, regardless of how trivial or even unrelated it may seem at the time" (Rodgers & Cowles, 1993, p. 222).

This directive to ultraspecification is at odds with the thrust of Sanjek's (1990a) "canon of fieldnote evidence [which] requires only that the relationship between fieldnotes and ethnography be made explicit. Ethnographic validity does not require extensive fieldnote documentation" (pp. 402-403; see also Emerson et al., 1995, p. ix). This directive is also at odds with the thrust of scientific method (Hammersley, 1997). As Bem (1987) counsels article authors, "Scientific integrity does not require you to lead your readers through all your wrongheaded hunches only to show— *voila!*—they were wrongheaded" (p. 173). This should apply to auditors as much it does to reviewers. It also applies, as it happens, to natural scientists, whose work really could and might be replicated.[69]

A fourth reason an audit would flounder is the perverse effect the prospect of auditing would have on record keeping. Not every ethnographer would regard his or her function, as Shulman (1994) does, as that of detective or spy. But all adept ethnographers amass a great many data that would be of partisan interest should they reach the eyes of insider cliques or outsider stakeholders. Not every ethnographer would be willing, as Scarce was, to spend months in a (U.S.) jail rather than reveal information about informants (see Scarce, 1994). But all ethnographers legitimately protect the privacy needs of both their informants and themselves.

In terms of ease of compliance with auditors' edicts, paradoxically, the least-skilled field researchers have the advantage. Faced with the prospect of creating an auditable paper trail, truly skilled ethnographers would mutate from inquirers into bureaucrats, attorneys, or both. As Hammersley (1997) argues, if researchers were to know that their notes and diaries would become public documents, these would cease to bear much connection to the real research process. Moreover, negotiating access to a site, seldom a trivial feat, would become vastly more difficult if the actors would, in effect, also be inviting in the auditors. The only virtue in archives, then, is the enabling of original research by collaborating researchers or carefully screened outsiders. Two legitimate uses by outsiders would be cross-cultural comparisons, as in the case of Human Relations Area Files researchers (discussed below), and the creation of new ethnographies, as in the case of Smith's use of Ella (Embree) Wiswell's notes on the women of Suye Mura (Smith, 1990).[70]

Tactics summary. The sad summary of the pursuit of objectivity is that the definition of the relevant research context is unknown. If defined, it could not be articulated fully; if it could, it could not be interpreted confidently. Full disclosure is just as chimerical a goal as complete neutrality on the part of the researcher. As Becker (1970, pp. 111, 123, 131) and Van Maanen (1991) have argued, the researcher cannot completely stand above the fray of factional and other interests. However, as with all of our epistemic frailties, this does not amount to a license to revel in our biases. Researchers can, and should, try to minimize biases, and they should try to disclose the critical sources of those biases.

There is no research method panacea that guarantees ethnographic objectivity. Nevertheless, there are several research method tactics that do help to improve a study's objectivity, and the most crucial of these, at least, should be used. Two of these tactics—the trail of the ethnographer's path and feedback from outsiders—are well suited to ethnographic inquiry, and help to mitigate the threats of bias on the part of both researchers and informants. Statistics-oriented interview techniques have the same effect, but are useful only for nonethnographic components of research projects. Two other tactics help marginally to mitigate the biases of the researcher (but not of informants): respondent validation and interrater checks on coding. One other tactic, the development of a comprehensive field database, has fatal limitations, except in certain cases of restudies and team-based research.

5. WORKING TOWARD PERSPICACITY

Perspicacity as a Goal

For qualitative methods, the conventional criterion of external validity or generalizability needs reconceptualization (Becker, 1990; Schofield, 1990). As we observed in the discussion of the ethnographer's path, ethnographers, *qua* ethnographers, do not and cannot use random sampling (see Behrens, 1990). Moreover, the face-to-face nature of their fieldwork engagements limits the number of actors who can be studied (Agar, 1996, p. 44). Behrens (1990) notes further that ethnographic data are spatially and temporally nonindependent, with distributions that are nonnormal and generally unknown. For these reasons, ethnographic findings cannot be used for statistical generalizations. But this does not mean that these findings could not "travel" without too much "stretching" (Sartori, 1970)—that is, "transfer" (Guba, 1981) to settings beyond the time and place of the field sites. Ethnographers not only could but should aspire to generate insights that can be *applied* elsewhere (Kidder, 1981; Lofland, 1995).

Ethnographers cannot aspire to generalizability or external validity, but they can aspire to perspicacity, which is the capacity to produce applicable insights. The plausibility of this criterion may be inferred from the well-institutionalized practice of applied anthropology. After all, the precondition for doing such work is, quite literally, that research results can be applied in more contexts than that of the microenvironment of fieldwork (Lyon, 1997). As Becker (1990) cautions, applied ethnographers may be goaded into generalizing wantonly to ad hoc constructs, such as business firms, of doubtful taxonomic validity. Like all ethnographers, they should instead aspire, first, to comprehend and to specify—dare one say to model?—the underlying or generic forms of interactions, processes, structures, and meanings, and second, to establish theoretically the domain in which these apply.[71]

An example of perspicacity: The matrilineal puzzle. As Schofield (1990) laments, perspicacity (literally, what she calls generalizability) has been favored by relatively little attention in the qualitative research literature. The attention it has received has tended to be, like my discussion thus far, rather abstract. An example would perhaps be something of a novelty, and it might prove to be instructive. The example I will serve up is Audrey Richards's (1950) assertion of "the matrilineal puzzle." I will indicate shortly why this example is fitting, but first, some explanation.

The matrilineal puzzle refers directly to a particular social structural challenge and indirectly to the range of resolutions created by the actors. The structural challenge is the conflict between the principles of exogamous marriage, descent through women (who, far from incidentally, bear the children) and male influence (if not outright dominance). The result of these principles is that, if a woman leaves the matrilineal group upon her marriage (in one solution to exogamy), her matrikin lose physical oversight of their heirs once she gives birth; if she brings her husband to her place of residence (in the other main solution), her brothers (the celebrated "mothers' brothers") disperse from the scene "where they have rights of succession" (Richards, 1950, p. 246; for a relentless presentation, see Fox, 1967, pp. 97, 111). Many resolutions to this problem revolve around residence rules, spatial proximity, and expectations about the husband's role.[72]

This example is apt, in that the matrilineal puzzle is hardly a "fact" that leaps out from the field at the researcher. (One should not infer here that the researcher monopolizes perspicacity; on the contrary, perspicacious informants are ardently to be sought out. Moreover, if it was one of Richards's informants who developed this construct with her, then that informant was effectively part of the research team; see Chapter 3.)

Richards appears to have developed her construct by means of intensive fieldwork in one setting (the Central African Bemba), familiarity with other Bantu peoples within the same "matrilineal belt" (Richards, 1950, p. 207), a deep awareness of a wide range of ethnographies, and comparative reflection. As Schlegel (1972) summarizes Richards's contribution, "Her typology was in the way of a pilot study . . . and the utility of her hypothesis about the matrilineal puzzle has been proven by the stimulus it has provided for other works" (p. 137). Her hypothesis, or construct, has been used and refined by later ethnographers working in different matrilineal societies (examples include Holy, 1986; Oppong, 1974). It has been tested and advanced by cross-cultural statistical analysis (Schlegel, 1972). It has, besides, served as a target for theoretical debates.[73] Not all perspicacious insights will necessarily prove to be so fecund as hers, but one can reasonably infer that an insight that has been so widely applied has definitely been perspicacious.

Inevitable Limits on Perspicacity

The ethnographer who seeks perspicacity seeks applicable insights. It follows that he or she faces two pivotal hurdles. First, the ethnographer has to come up with an insight. Next, he or she has to show how to apply this insight somewhere else. Because of this second requirement, perspicacity transcends description and veracity, aiming instead at nonobvious understandings of the sort that become apparent as a rule only with analysis. Perspicacity is similar to Wolcott's (1994, p. 367, chap. 11) criterion of "understanding," which is his term to substitute for *validity.* Understanding appears to be a concept, somewhat like validity, that subsumes both dimensions of perspicacity: insight rooted in veracity (analogous to internal validity) and conceptual traveling or applicability (analogous to external validity).

In the Richards (1950) example, the *insight* was a structural puzzle; the *application* was to matrilineal systems. For the first challenge, of being insightful, a method text such as this one can offer only partial assistance. We have observed (in Chapter 2) that this is a reason many ethnographers discount the value of method: The generation of insights transcends mere technique. This critique is warranted so far as it goes, but there are research method tactics that help to catalyze the effort. Moreover, tactics that facilitate veracity and objectivity might also help to spark insights. I have already presented the example of perspicacious informants; other tactics, such as lengthy fieldwork, reorienting observations, and apprenticeship roles, are also candidates for this function.

For the second perspicacity challenge, research tactics are more directly helpful, because they facilitate the effort to delineate the findings so as to clarify when and where they apply. In principle, ethnographers resolve these questions by means of iterative comparisons within and beyond their fieldwork data. This is why Hammersley (1990, pp. 98-99) invokes, as a means toward theoretical generalization, the tactic of seeking out reorienting or disconfirming observations. With this means, researchers specify the myriad contingencies that do and do not qualify their findings.

The challenge of taxonomy. Unfortunately, these ethnographic efforts at comparison are seriously corrupted by one of the most vexing dilemmas in social science. I have cited Becker (1990) above on the folly of using folk classifications to determine the category for which a finding applies. In his example, *school* refers to a folk category, not to a taxonomic unit. In the matrilineal puzzle example, Richards's critic Leach (1961, chap. 1) disputes the classificatory validity of matriliny. Although he may have been "unfair" in his critique of Richards (Schlegel, 1972, p. 139), he was right to target tautological and arbitrary typologies. Taxonomy is a "prerequisite" of both generalization (Mandel, 1996, chap. 1) and the use of scientific methods (McKelvey, 1982, p. 3). As Whyte (1984) remarks, "advances" in biology "have depended particularly upon shifting from conventional or common sense classifications to systems more useful for scientific research" (p. 270). Lacking such a basis, an ethnographic "comparison depends on inferred rather than obvious similarities," with the result that "the question of external validity [in our terms, applicability] . . . is never completely answerable" (Kidder, 1981, p. 253).

Taxonomic deficiencies would be less debilitating, and folk comparisons less deceptive, were it not for a property of empirically derived taxonomies known as *polythetism* (Bailey, 1973; Needham, 1975). Folk taxonomies tend to have clearly delineated, monothetic boundaries between taxa (i.e., real populations of a distinct type). However, empirical studies in biology and in social science demonstrate the fuzziness that characterizes polythetic boundaries.[74] With polythetic taxa, no feature is sufficient by its presence to assign a member to a taxon, and members of a taxon need not display all diacritical features. Taken together, these properties have nasty implications for research. Taxa overlap and display "sporadic resemblances" (Needham, 1975, pp. 351-352). Further, polythetic taxonomies render the nomothetic comparative method "more daunting and perhaps even unfeasible" (Needham, 1975, p. 358). They violate the "scholastic" or monothetic "substitution principle" (Needham, 1975, p. 361), whereby what is known about one member of a taxon is also known about the others.[75]

This boundary delineation problem has proven one of the most obdurate of the challenges in statistical efforts at cross-cultural comparison. The most persistent, thoughtful, and sophisticated of the efforts to overcome these challenges is that of the Human Relations Area Files (HRAF).[76] Barnes (1971) notes one of the main HRAF conundrums, that "even the simplest [statistical] statements . . . have no meaning unless the units that are added up are equivalent to one another" (p. 67). "In cross-cultural research, this challenge is severely compounded by questions of diffusion [of cultural traits], population size [differences], and—thorniest of all—

boundary delineation (Barnes, 1971, pp. 66-72; Van Maanen, 1988, p. 21). This [categorizing] challenge is related to the challenge of context" (Stewart, Learned, Mandel, & Peterson, 1995, p. 177).

Statistically oriented field researchers, such as Aunger (1994, 1995), seek to tease out the effects of "elements that are [in] common" across research moments (1995, p. 113). From an ethnographic perspective, this abstraction removes the observations from the systemic context that constitutes their meaning (Frayser, 1996; Ragin, 1987; Strathern, 1987). As Abbott counters, Aunger assumes that the elicitation effects of kinship, status, and so on are "separable," whereas they "are all bound together" (Abbott, commentary in Aunger, 1995, p. 115). For this reason, "it makes more sense to try to group different types of individuals." That is, Abbott's suggested solution is taxonomic. As the example of the matrilineal puzzle illustrates (Schlegel, 1972, p. 138), conceptual traveling in ethnography rests on comparison of, at best, polythetically (more or less) similar contexts or systems.

The challenges that confront structural or synchronic comparisons are daunting enough. They are all the more daunting in the case of process or diachronic comparisons. Thanks in good measure to the HRAF enterprise, if one wishes to try one's hand at the synchronic comparison of structures or of systems, one can rely on a cumulation of methodological know-how embodied in books and articles (such as Ember & Ember, 1997; Murdock et al., 1987; Naroll, 1970b), a journal (*Cross-Cultural Research*), a Web site (www.yale.edu/hraf/home.htm), and, of course, the "files" themselves (which amount to a massive indexed record of worldwide ethnographic materials).[77]

If one wishes to try one's hand not at synchronic comparisons but at diachronic comparisons of processes, one should prepare to do a little trailblazing. Granted, there are grounds for optimism. Sociologists such as Abbott, Abell, and Heise have worked at devising procedures to compare patterns among events over time (see Abbott, 1992, 1997; Griffin, 1992; Morse, 1998, chap. 2). Still, these techniques have only begun to be used to systematize the temporal patterns that are depicted in ethnographies. This lacuna in analysis applies even to avowedly processual ethnographies, whether these are long-term cultural anthropology projects (Foster et al., 1979) or the Rhodes-Livingstone-Manchester model of "extended case" ethnographies (Van Velsen, 1967). Thus, if one wishes to make process comparisons, one can count on coping without the benefit of an inventory of temporal patterns, let alone a taxonomy of processual classes.[78]

Research Coping Tactics

TACTIC 1: INTENSE CONSIDERATION
OF THE DATA

Data manipulation—what Wolcott (1994) would call the analytic aspect of data transformation—can become more efficient, more consistent, and even more disciplined with the use of well-established procedures and current computer technologies. However, the only assurance that can be justified *exclusively on the basis of the method of data manipulation* is that objectivity has been served by means of the specification of procedure. There are two reasons that more ringing assurances would not in a literal sense be true. First, all modes of research involve judgment calls and offer opportunities to manipulate the outcomes (Fox, 1994; Goodstein, 1991). Second, in ethnography, the means by which the data are considered cannot be specified completely. The reason for this is not so much the complexity of the process as the impossibility of distinguishing it fully from the socially embedded, emergent process of learning that is, at heart, what ethnography is. From beginning to end, inquiry is characterized by non-linear cycles of comparisons[79] between units of data and a range of other mental activities, including observation, labeling, indexing, reflections on various literatures and cases, memoing, and incipient theorizing (Agar, 1991). The consideration of ethnographic data is entangled in an idiosyncratic and "crooked route" (Seidel et al., 1988, p. 3-10; see also Bailyn, 1977).

Therefore, from a rigorous or auditing perspective, the means of using data should have been included in the previous chapter. However, one cannot make prescriptions for method without making the assumption of good faith on the part of the researcher. Good faith is required for any method tactic to achieve its objectives, in ethnography or any mode of inquiry. If one does assume self-discipline on the part of the researcher, it can then be claimed that data manipulation procedures also help in efforts at veracity. They are directly very helpful for that purpose by facilitating the search for disconfirmations. Their capacity to be specified is helpful in efforts at objectivity. These procedures facilitate the record of the ethnographer's path and help the conscientious researcher in the pursuit of perspicacity.

Inspiration and perspiration. Procedures for the consideration of data are beneficial in serving the interests of veracity and objectivity. They are virtually essential for most of the ethnographer's efforts to achieve perspicacity. Penetrating insights may erupt as inspirations, but they do so only after the ethnographer has expended a great deal of effort. That effort takes the inquirer down the "crooked" data manipulation route (Seidel et al., p. 3-10) that wends its way through "numerous cycles" (Agar, 1991, p. 193) in which the curious stop, like pilgrims, to "confront lots of [potential explanations and] theories with relatively small amounts of data" (Gerson, 1989, p. 412).

Decontextualizing, memoing, and recontextualizing. Readying the data for these intensive confrontations requires that the ethnographer invest time in up-front planning and data management (Werner & Schoepfle, 1987, vol. 2, p. 267). In this preparation, the initial task of indexing and coding prepares the way for the next processes, which will be referred to as *decontextualizing, memoing,* and *recontextualizing* (following Sanjek, 1990a; Schensul, 1993; Tesch, 1990, p. 251).

The semichaos of the process of ethnographic work with data and concepts can be simplified through a focus on the chronic core cycle of decontextualizing, memoing, and recontextualizing. Let us assume, as economists say, that to ease the task (the ethnographer's and mine), data management software has been used, and that a careful effort has been made to read and index the field notes. These preliminaries help to advance the development of theory (Richards & Richards, 1994). For some ethnographers, this step toward understanding is more valuable than later efforts at data retrieval (Emerson et al., 1995, pp. 151, 230 n. 3).[80] However, data consideration becomes more systematic with the downstream stage, which Seidel et al. (1988) call "decontextualization."

Decontextualization is executed by computer searches for segments in the record that are tagged with selected index words. The creators of the Ethnograph software explain that this "is the point where you remove things that you have noticed in your data from their original context, and put them in a new context: the context of all similar things" (Seidel et al., 1988, p. 9-1). *Decontextualization* refers to the recombining of data segments according to shared index words rather than their remaining, say, inserted as the 58th to 85th lines of notes on a ceremony observed in March, and the 303rd to 312th lines of the text of a speech event recorded in April. This does not mean that the trail to the primary context is lost. Even in this stage of abstracting the data, a great deal of the original segment's context should be, and is, retained. In the example of an Ethnograph search, the time, place, speaker and other actors, exact file location, and potentially other details are retained (Seidel et al., 1988, pp. 9-29; Tesch, 1990, pp. 251, 264).[81]

First-order constructs, as reflected by "open" codes and index words, apply to anything ethnographers notice in their data. Moreover, their data should be, as I have noted in Chapter 2, comprehensive. Consequently, the full set of index words is, at worst, a morass; at best, it is an inchoate guide for depiction or for theory development. As Emerson et al. (1995) remind us, "The ultimate goal is to produce," out of this conceptual sprawl, "a coherent, focused analysis of some aspect of the social life that has been observed" (p. 142). This calls for "selecting core themes" (p. 157) from the tangle of topics that, unweeded, would sprout from the data.

Like everything else in the ethnographic process, topical focus is achieved iteratively, with frequent reflections on prior theories, the data, concepts these data inspire, and (again and again) the data. Throughout these efforts, the researcher writes down emergent ideas about analysis and interpretation, in the form of occasional asides, commentaries, and memos (Emerson et al., 1995, p. 100; Strauss, 1987, pp. 81, 127). Once these ideas appear promising, the researcher is ready for *recontextualization*. In this stage, the ethnographer's goal is to advance empirical inquiry and theorizing by refocusing the selected data on an "inclusive" theme that he or she has crafted and selected as particularly important (Emerson et al., 1995, p. 159).[82]

The ethnographer does this by developing second-order indexing. Second-order indexing differs from first-order indexing in two ways. First, it is tailored to the new context, which is the primary theme or line of inquiry. Such themes are based on reflections on first-order index words, but they may well not have occurred to the researcher during open, first-order indexing. Second, this indexing produces constructs that cut across, prioritize, and cluster the first-order index words and codes. An illustration may make this clearer. (I call it an *illustration* because *example* would connote the representative or typical, and I do not know, and doubt that anyone knows, what typical practice may be. It is, however, somewhat consoling to notice that the outline of my illustration is similar to that of the process prescribed by Emerson et al., 1995, pp. 159-160.)

In the case in question, I was studying interrelationships among social network monopolization, resource creation, and autocratic control in an entrepreneurial firm (Stewart & Krackhardt, 1997). In order to work toward Emerson et al.'s (1995) goal of a "coherent, focused analysis" (p. 142), and to retain the sociocultural description and sensitivity to site-specific context that characterize an ethnographic "tale" (Van Maanen, 1988), I needed to order my data in a way that was different from what searches of first-order index words alone would allow. One theme of the tale, in this case, is the way the entrepreneur resolves conflicts with employees such that his or her "good puppies" are retained as employees and his rivals for the entrepreneurial role are not. This theme, as in much ethnography, incorporates both narrative description and also a gateway into a third-order construct—in this case, labor market power that is used to preserve an entrepreneur's position as entrepreneur.

Constructs like this are more synthesizing and complex than those that I, given my limitations, could hope to notice at the stage of open indexing. It was derived only after I had considered a set of second-order constructs, none of which was itself immediately apparent. For example, one of these second-order constructs was the ways in which Pinky controls and social-izes his employees. The file I created on that construct was based on a bundle of index words that included COMMAND, (operating) CONTROL, COPY, DISCIPLINE, EXHORT, INSTRUCT, LEADER, LEGITIMATE, MANAGEMENT_PHILOSOPHY, NORM, STIR, and TRAIN. None of these, in itself, would have been sufficient to retrieve the second-order, let alone third-order, story.

With guidance from my integrative memos, I patched this second-order story together with data segments that were selected from Ethnograph searches. These searches retrieved the data tagged by index words that had been chosen, prioritized, and clustered on the basis of their relevance for this particular topical focus. The second-order constructs then resided, as it were, not in sets of index and code words and their definitions (like first-order constructs), or in webs of concepts, subconcepts, and dimensions (like grounded theories), but rather in their own computer files. This is because the Ethnograph and similar software lets one print the results of searches to disk, where data can then be culled, reordered, or shuffled from file to file with the use of a word processor.[83]

What should be documented? Formal techniques of data manipulation, as embodied in software, are very handy for first-order, second-order, and, for that matter, any-order indexing and sorting of the data. However, data consideration also depends, even more substantially, on tacit knowledge and creative insight.[84] Therefore, the ethnographer could document only a part, the formal and explicit part, of the story. Although this is certainly a serious qualification, the formal part of this story does merit formal attention.

The method discussion should include documentation of the data consideration process, but how much detail should be included? If the main objective is to legitimate ethnography in the eyes of conventional researchers, the more the merrier. After all, this discussion has assumed the use of sophisticated-sounding computer techniques. However, if the main objective is to describe the route to perspicacity, fairly simple documentation will serve the purpose nicely.[85] (The exceptions would be nonethnographic uses of ethnography, such as HRAF studies, and, perhaps, those truly extraordinary circumstances that require attempts at later replication.)

Currently, expectations are ill defined for documenting either data consideration or, as Sanjek (1990a) puts it, "the relationship of fieldnotes to ethnographic text" (p. 402). Sanjek adduces Agar's (1986a) *Independents Declared* as an exemplar, and Agar's depiction (pp. 178-179) is admittedly more explicit than most. However, it is still rather vague, referring only to the number of transcript pages, number of data segments (Ethnograph code sets)—a rough measure of intensity of indexing—and the percentage of these data that were used in the analysis.

Reviewers should, generally, expect to find an *outline* of the procedures used for decontextualizing, memoing, and recontextualizing. How, for example, were index or code words prioritized and clustered in the creation of higher-order constructs? Were recontextualized constructs intended to be largely descriptive, largely conceptual, or both? Reviewers with a markedly skeptical, or auditing, mentality might also wish to see what methods were used in the pursuit of disconfirming or reorienting observations. Reviewers and diligent readers should also be given the chance to know about significant index and code words.

Full details would take too much room for the method section, but they could be provided in alternative venues. An appendix, or a Web site perhaps, could be used to publish the complete set of index and code words, along with their definitions. This document also could list the number of data segments per index or code word; could indicate if terms were used as index words, code words, or both; and could distinguish terms that were emergent and grounded from those that were a priori and literature-based.

Theoretical candor. The rationale for much of this specification is the canon that Sanjek (1990a) calls "theoretical candor" (pp. 395-398).[86] By this, Sanjek means making explicit the principles and practices of theoretical sampling. What level of detail would be required to realize this goal? Certain authors appear to hold that the "complete network" of concepts (Hammersley's term) needs to be detailed (see Brewer, 1994; Hammersley,

1990, pp. 75-78; Werner & Schoepfle, 1987, vol. 1, pp. 312, 316, 335). One can only interpret their prescription to mean *in the body of the write-up.* In the method discussion, theoretical sampling can be documented quite adequately at the level of detail just covered—that is, the categories of data and the major concepts used, and the outline of the process in which higher-order constructs were created. This should suffice. Ethnographic analysis is an engagement of ideas and those segments of data that are sampled with these ideas in mind, and the inverse engagement. The segments of data—the objects for contemplation—as well as the concepts that are brought to bear in this effort are, equally, enmeshed and manifested in the ordered pattern of the index terms that are invoked in the consideration of data.

Comparisons with other ethnographies. The concepts that are brought to bear in these cycles may have been derived from or inspired by sundry sources, including idiosyncratic personal experience. For purposes of method explication, however, the manifold scholarly literatures are sufficiently diverse to incorporate most of these concepts. Therefore, for most purposes, theoretical candor is served by citations to the literature in the body of the write-up. In ethnographic writing, this scholarly custom provides credit not only to the particular authors cited but also to the constitutive role of literature-based comparison in ethnographic inquiry.[87]

TACTIC 2: EXPLORATION

Consideration of the literature is a staple of postfieldwork "sampling." At least that is how statistics-oriented researchers would see it. If they were to examine the ethnographer's use of data, they would say that any item selected for consideration—whether a field note observation, memory, data from a published study, theoretical construct, or mental experiment (March, Sproull, & Tamuz, 1991)—has, on that account, been sampled. That would be true but misleading. *Statistics-oriented researchers "sample," pursuing representation. Ethnographers "explore," pursuing discovery.*

People explore by doggedly rooting out what interests them. Exploration is a quest; it is not a technique that lends itself to tidy or comprehensive prescriptions. Nevertheless, exploration is not idiographic. A discovery that is interesting only in its own setting's terms—that is, a purely idiographic finding—might very well be insightful. However, it could not be perspicacious, because it would lack applicability. For the same reason, it could not really be "interesting." As Davis (1971) and Weick (1979, pp. 51-60) explain, an interesting assertion disrupts the readership's assumptions. These assumptions are reconfigured, but they are neither obliterated (in which case the assertion would be dismissed as absurd) nor disregarded (in which case the assertion would be dismissed as irrelevant).

Because the quest that concerns us is a quest for applicable, interesting insights, it is not entirely idiosyncratic. It cannot be routinized, but its outlines can be sketched. To sketch those outlines, albeit incompletely, I turn first to the problem of selecting the locus of exploration—the field site—and the challenge of thinking through just where any insights derived at this field site could travel. Second, I address the problem of selecting which of the objects of exploration—the findings—ought to be reported.

Site selection. Ethnographic exploration gets its initial bearings with the choice of a field site in which to study. Katz (1997) observes scornfully that this choice may tend to be made after the fact: "Often, after entering a field site for any number of extraneous reasons (e.g., family connections, the need to make money) and gathering data without a clear guiding definition of the substantive issues, an ethnographer would identify a social process for which the site just happened to be a brilliantly strategic data source" (p. 412). Fair enough; it *would* be comforting if explorers knew where they were trying to go. However, as Weick (1979) asserts, the typical sequence in human cognition is "action precedes thought" (p. 194). Moreover, prescience is not a prerequisite of discovery—far from it, if one can extrapolate from ethnographic practice, where opportunism often proves to be the canny strategy.[88]

There may not even be any way to decide, prior to entry into the field, where one ought to try to go. March et al. (1991) contend that "we do not have a shared conception of . . . what distinguishes single cases that are informative from those that are not" (p. 10). In ethnography and case research, there may actually exist a "shared conception" that offers both guidance prior to entry and a basis for evaluation after the fact. The problem is not so much the absence of such a conception as it is the limited capacity to translate it into rules that, prior to entry, would enable the evaluation of alternative sites.

Most site selection criteria promote the interests of "exploration" in the intuitive sense of uncovering new knowledge. One such example is the site's potential to reveal the "ideal or exceptional" (Schofield, 1990, pp. 217-221). Similarly, case researchers are advised to search for "extreme or unique" and "revelatory" sites (Yin, 1984, p. 43; emphasis removed). In seeking such sites, ethnographers need to consider not only the location but also the timing (Gersick, 1994) that will provide chances to witness social dramas and critical incidents (Pettigrew, 1990; Turner, 1957).

Mitchell (1974) expresses the underlying principle of exploring for social dramas and exceptional events in arguing that ethnographers should seek out sites that are "so idiosyncratic as to throw into sharp relief the principles underlying them" (p. 204). Similarly, in Geertz's (1976) familiar formulation, the ethnographer's goal is "to grasp concepts which, for another people, are experience-near, and to do so well enough to place them in illuminating connection with experience-distant concepts theorists have fashioned to capture the general features of social life" (p. 224). Such connections are the foundations of an ethnography's perspicacity, in the sense of its capacity to generate potentially transferable insight.

Some site selection criteria promote the interests of "exploration" in the more limited and counterintuitive sense of renewed exploration of extant theories or constructs. For example, one favorable property of a site is the prospect for the restudy of an earlier ethnography (Johnson, 1990). I have maintained that it would be futile to conduct a restudy if the primary purpose is objectivity (see note 36). However, it would not be futile if the purpose is veracity, in cases where one can pick up again on the trail of reorienting observations. Such a restudy (or, one would better say, reinvestigation) would also enhance perspicacity, in the sense of clarifying a construct's extension or applicability.

A closely related motive for selecting a site is its potential for disconfirming observations. Research in such a site could be a "crucial case test" (Eckstein, 1975/1992, pp. 152-163) of an existing theory. (Yin, 1984, calls this a "critical case test"; p. 42.) There are two preconditions for crucial case testing. First, the theory must be sufficiently "well-formulated" (Yin, 1984, p. 42) or "ruleful" (Eckstein, 1975/1992, p. 157) that it is possible to define disconfirming observations. Second, the site must have the full set of features that, according to the theory, would undoubtedly be expected to conform, or undoubtedly not to conform, to the theoretical predictions (see also Ragin, 1987, p. 52).[89]

Searching for contingencies. Ethnographers determine where to apply their insights by iteratively specifying the contingencies that apply for their cases and comparing these with other cases, insights, and theorized contingencies. In the discussion of the first exploration tactic, data consideration, this process was presented largely as a matter of technique. Such a presentation ignores the need for the ethnographer to *explore* in order to find the applicable points of comparison. These points can be discovered by three routes. The first is within-site theoretical sampling. The second is reflections on the literature, or, as I have termed this elsewhere, the use of "library tales" (Stewart, 1990). When these handier routes have been exhausted, the final recourse is to conduct new fieldwork in astutely selected field sites.

Within-site theoretical sampling has been considered thus far in this book as an active search for reorienting and disconfirming observations, and for breakdowns of old understandings. Perhaps these breakdowns should be called, in this context, *epiphanies*. It happens that ethnographic epiphanies (like any others) are not in boundless supply. From a methodological perspective, they are facilitated by the selection of a field site with the "maximum variation" on phenomena of interest.[90] However, the inquisitive ethnographer will find eventually that the observable variation is fully consumed. (It is assumed here that the ethnographer cares to "abstract . . . valid models of complex phenomena which show [much] local variability"—an assumption that Barth [1989, p. 125] would consider overly optimistic.)

A site might encompass variation on a wide range of contingencies, including, say, religious affiliation, household income, levels of political involvement, and incorporation into the global economy. However, it might have no variation at all in, say, its modes of ecological adaptation or its governmental and tax regime. Variation on these locally invariant dimensions can be acquired, most efficiently, through explorations in the library (Glaser & Strauss, 1967, p. 176). As Rosenblatt (1981) observes, library comparisons expand the limited "within-culture comparative material" available to the ethnographer (p. 218). However, as Glaser and Strauss (1967, pp. 180-183) recognize, these comparisons will almost certainly not be tailored sufficiently for all theory-building requirements. They can probably be extended somewhat by means of the Human Relations Area Files, but these too have limitations (Stewart et al., 1995). If ethnographers are to find specifically customized observations, often they will have to do primary research themselves.

For some purposes, ethnographers might extend the range of observations by conducting historical research (Comaroff & Comaroff, 1992; Lewis, 1968). However, historical documents, if they prove to be available at all, may be just as unlikely as published ethnographies to include the particular, detailed contingencies of interest. Differences in data may be one of the reasons historians paint on a much bigger canvas—a "mural," Geertz (1990, p. 322) has called it—than the "miniature" (Geertz again) of ethnographers. If they still wish to extend the trail of reorienting and disconfirming observations, they may have little option other than do-it-yourself observation in multiple field sites.

This is the rationale both for "matched comparison" studies and for case replication research. Multiple-site case research is an apparently similar option that has been recommended by several writers.[91] However, ethnographers have seldom followed that advice. Wolcott (1994) articulates the ethnographer's riposte: "The risk in conducting fieldwork at multiple sites is to forgo the opportunity to produce one well-contextualized qualitative study in the course of producing an inadequate quantitative one" (p. 182). As Schofield (1990) make this argument, multiple-site research is expensive and time-consuming, trading off intensive understanding in favor of coverage that is wider, but still fails to yield a statistically meaningful n. If the question one wishes to answer is the distribution question, the conclusion is that one needs to conduct or use a survey (Agar, 1996, p. 46).

These are valid critiques of multiple-site efforts at statistical generalization. These are not valid critiques of matched comparisons or case replications. The objective of these more modest modes of multiple-site study is the extension of exploration. Both of these modes are means of continuing a specified trail of inquiry into other sites. These other sites should be selected either to improve maximally on single-site variation or to maximize the potential for disconfirmation. The catch with these efforts follows directly from these desiderata. It is difficult first to identify and then to secure access to restrictively defined—hence, as a rule, rare—field sites (Stewart, 1990).

Reporting of Detail Relevant for Theory, Comparison, and Practice

At some point, even the most persistent of field-workers stop their exploring, or at least they switch their focus to what they can discover while in the process of writing. At this stage, what should they document about the exploration process? Customarily, even the most cursory method discussions have addressed the field site. Treatments have tended to be descriptive, along the lines of "For 17 months, the author conducted participant observation among the Bongo Wongo, the secret society of Canadian stockbrokers." Discussions should (and generally would) further indicate if the design included a restudy, matched pair or multiple sites, or a crucial case test. Special efforts to track down illuminating literature, such as the use of HRAF files, could also be recognized. Beyond that, explorations are generally, and properly, left to their reflections in the findings. There would hardly be a need for method discussions—or for this book—if ethnographic method equaled exploration.

What explorers manage to uncover has immeasurably more consequence than the means they have used for their exploring. This distinction ought to be repeated when auditors and other methodologists issue their edicts for specification: It is not the process of discovery that matters, but what has been discovered. An ethnographer would not have needed to have studied among the Bemba at midcentury, let alone follow Audrey Richards's precise ethnographer's path, to have independently discerned the matrilineal puzzle.

This principle applies to laboratory scientists as well. If another lab had managed to replicate Pons and Fleischmann's claims about cold fusion with somewhat different methods, those claims would still have been supported (Johnson, 1990, pp. 15-16). Differences in details would, in that case, have precipitated some rethinking, because findings in laboratory science are very tightly coupled with procedure. A major difference in ethnography is that its findings—at least those interesting findings that transcend the merely descriptive—are very loosely coupled with procedure. The reason is that creativity and the overdetermination of pattern and method are prerequisites of ethnographic perspicacity.

If perspicacity is overdetermined, the question arises of which details on the discoveries are worth reporting. A widely accepted answer is the Geertzian prescription of "thick description." [92] When this expression is (usefully) defined as "that [description] which maximizes the use of discrepant ethnographic images for deeper ethnographic understanding" (Werner & Schoepfle, 1987, vol. 2, p. 312), it still remains too vague to guide the author (Reyna, 1994). Maximal variation is fine in the data, but not, in all its details, in the report. Further guidance requires an answer to the question, How is it that thick description might be supportive of perspicacity?

I have quoted Geertz himself, a couple dozen paragraphs above, with the first of three possible solutions. Geertz's (1976) answer is the connection to be drawn between observations and "experience-distant concepts . . . [that] capture the general features of social life" (p. 224). Perspicacity is supported not by reams of Boasian details, but by *theorized* details. But now, one may ask, how should one decide which theories to use? The cynical answer (noted, not advocated, by Aldrich et al., 1994) is to focus on theories currently in fashion in the journals. A better answer, according to proponents of the thick description solution, is to focus on theories that best help to determine where a certain insight can travel (Schofield, 1990).

This solution applies to the theory development of the ethnographer but also of the readers, who can use the report as a library tale for their own explorations. Thus, the perspicacity advanced by a write-up need not be the ethnographer's own. This point applies equally to the second solution to the "which details?" question. Ethnographers should report in detail on all the contingencies that inhere in or affect their proffered constructs and theories. This detail should enable potential reconstruction or disconfirmation by other scholars' reinvestigations. Thus, ethnographies should be able to "claim . . . that no negative case can be found [that has not been accounted for, and thus the report should invite] the testing of findings without repeating the original research. A subsequent researcher [should be able to] pick up where the study left off, looking for a single contradiction" (Katz, 1983, p. 145).

For the third solution to the "which details?" question, the perspicacity to be advanced is entirely that of the readers. As Noblit and Hare (1988, chap. 4) represent this solution, an ethnography should offer enough detail that other scholars, with alternative perspectives, can "translate" the findings and theories so as to make them their own. One way to oblige is to refer, throughout the entire research process, to the comprehensive checklists of the *Outline of Cultural Materials* (Murdock et al., 1987; for cultural anthropologists) or the *Notes and Queries on Anthropology* (Royal Anthropological Institute, 1951; for social anthropologists). As Moran (1995) acknowledges, both of these publications have long seemed "curious and somewhat archaic" to many ethnographers (p. 3). Certainly, it might seem eccentric to publish reports titled, say, "Salt" or "String Figures and Tricks" (Royal Anthropological Institute, 1951). But possibly not. Moreover, it would be very hard to argue that quite enough is known already about "lineage and class," "law and justice," "consumption," or "ritual beliefs concerned with economic activities."

Using a particular checklist is considerably less critical in this solution than an orientation in favor of disclosure. Becker (1986, pp. 130-131) has suggested "that ethnographies are sometimes treated by sociological theorists as mere 'files to be ransacked' for answers to questions the fieldworker may well deem inappropriate" (cited by Van Maanen, 1988, p. 30). Becker's complaint is valid, if what he laments is the loss of contextualized meaning attendant on sociological abstractions. However, Moran (1995) is also on target in holding that, if ethnographers prove unwilling to submit findings for use by the wider social science community, they "gradually marginalize" their explorations. "If I feel any frustration at all with the qualitative endeavor," Wolcott (1994) writes, "it is that the completed studies are not well, or well enough, used" (p. 416). Ethnographers stand a much higher chance of their studies being used if they demonstrate a willingness to give generously, comprehensively, and eclectically of their results.

Tactics summary. Reviewers and other readers with a quantitative orientation will, presumably, gravitate toward discussions of the formal techniques that are used for data analysis. By now there should be little doubt that this tactic is a secondary ingredient in the ethnographic recipe for insights. One could even admit (as I have above) that some of the ethnographer's discussions of this tactic might be more effective in attaining external legitimacy than in explaining very much about perspicacity. Enough of these apologies, however; with the tactics I have recommended, my conscience is clear. Intense consideration of data and exploration matter. They may be incapable of compelling insights, but they can be used to encourage creativity and to expedite conceptual traveling. The first tactic, intense consideration of data, promotes the iterative consideration and comparison—of units of data, other cases, and concepts—that in turn facilitate insight and enable the researcher to navigate to those times and places where the insight should travel. The other tactic, exploration, pertains to probing for data and potential observations, and for theories and ethnographic writings that are invoked for consideration.

6. PUTTING EXPECTATIONS TO USE

An Editorial and Funding Review
Checklist for Ethnographic Method

In Chapter 1, in an effort to vindicate the mandate for this book, I argued that ethnographers are disadvantaged, relative to partisans of other forms of qualitative research, by their lack of a set of method standards of their own. I made no explicit promises that this book would institute a canon akin to, say, what Glaser and Strauss (1967) provided grounded theory. Possibly so, but surely I dropped some hints to that effect. One way to help make good on any implied promise is to summarize, in an appendix, the canon that has been cobbled together. This summary adopts a format, the method components of a reviewer's checklist (Campion, 1993b), that could help beat a trail for ethnography—*ethnography,* not reinvented in the image of conventional research—through the tangles of funding and editorial review.

The version of the Editorial and Funding Review Checklist for Ethnographic Method presented in the Appendix to this volume incorporates three examples of the checklist's usage. Examples are presented of answers to the checklist's questions for Gouldner's *Patterns of Industrial Bureaucracy* (1954; see Van Maanen, 1988, pp. 54, 142), Barker's "Tightening the Iron Cage: Concertive Control in Self-Managing Teams" (1993), and Kondo's *Crafting Selves* (1990). Barker's work is a relatively recent foray into perspicacity that is, like Gouldner's, a Weberian take on the topic of employees' legitimation of organizational regimes. Kondo provides a feminist take on the same topic. Agar (1996) uses Kondo's book as the exemplar of "a 'new' ethnography" (p. 7); I use it here to see if the checklist holds up for writers, like Kondo, who create works that (in my view) are very fine but that do not fly the "flag" of science (Van Maanen, 1995, p. 73). Such authors could argue that the expectations proposed in this book do not apply in their cases. Kondo's case suggests, one could argue, that such works are also amenable to the checklist's treatment.

The checklist refers specifically to the methods of these studies, and not to other factors (such as writing quality, empathy, or insight) that are likely determinants of perceived impact or value. Method is a necessary, but not a sufficient, contributor to the caliber of an ethnography. At least that has been my assumption in this book. In a now-familiar assertion (familiar at least for its opening clause), Malinowski (1922/1961) apparently holds that method is not only necessary, but also sufficient, for an ethnography's contribution. He asks, "What is then this ethnographer's magic, by which he is able to evoke the real spirit of the natives, the true picture of tribal life?" He answers, "As usual, success can only be obtained by a patient and systematic application of a number of rules of common sense and well-known scientific principles . . . the principles of method" (p. 6).

Rhetorical fancy may well be at play in this passage, but not as much as it might at first appear. For what are these "principles of method" at stake here? Following Malinowski's own depiction, they are those of "effective fieldwork" (p. 6; see also pp. 7-15). The principles that Malinowski enunciates amount to those, and only those, that undergird the core activities that engender understanding between researchers and insiders. Their "application" is the mindful deployment of tactics—involved participation, the active pursuit and consideration of comprehensive data and comparative ideas—that facilitate this foundational function of learning.

Does Malinowski overstate the importance of research method in affecting the quality of ethnographies? One way to answer this question is to examine how well the checklist succeeds in flagging the contributions and limitations of particular examples. All three examples used in the checklist make a persuasive case for interesting findings. For example, Gouldner (1954) is insightful on the relationships between contexts, including management succession, and modalities of bureaucracy. Barker (1993) is insightful on contexts, including corporate growth, and the emergence of formalization in team-based organization. Kondo (1990, pp. 111-112) is insightful, for example, on the way that rituals of resocialization incorporate or co-opt resistance and skepticism on the part of participants. The evidence in the checklist is consistent with perspicacity on the part of these writings.

None of these studies is based on sophisticated methods of data analysis, but all show signs of data thought through in depth. All show signs of fieldwork conducted so as to allow the researcher to encounter meaningful variations and doggedly search out possibilities. All make good scholarly use of other writings. Moreover, all lay a solid basis for perspicacity in veracity and objectivity.[93] Gouldner and Barker, unlike Kondo, have a need to compensate for brief periods of fieldwork and marginal participation. The checklist shows that they use different tactics for this purpose. For example, Gouldner uses the unofficial collaboration of a strategically located insider, and Barker his own related experience. Both are based on fieldwork in sites amenable to quick bursts of fieldwork and offering exceptional prospects for within-site comparisons. Like Kondo, both make good use of outsider feedback. These strengths and weaknesses in Gouldner's and Barker's works suggest, quite correctly, that they fall on the grounded theory, or "thin," end of the ethnographic spectrum. Consequently, some apprehensions endure about the exhaustiveness of these researchers' empirical efforts to disconfirm their assertions. However, Gouldner and Barker express their key propositions sufficiently clearly that they could be disconfirmed with a reinvestigation.

Kondo's work illustrates that what is engaging in ethnographies may not necessarily transfer swiftly to other contexts and, hence, need not meet the criteria for perspicacity. Kondo argues explicitly that "experience and evocation can *become theory*," and demonstrates this point, at least to my satisfaction, with her own experiences (pp. 8, 24). Thus, theoretical presentations can have weakly developed connections with testable assertions and yet be of interest. *Crafting Selves* serves as a caution against a strictly methodological assessment. Still, the checklist does draw attention to vital method strengths of the book, and particularly to Kondo's use of her own multiple role involvements, which precipitate epiphanies on the socially situated nature of identity formation. It is ironic, given this strength, that the main limitation of the book, also apparent from the checklist, is a rather fragmented depiction of the contexts and identities of actors other than Kondo herself.

In all three cases, other inquirers could disconfirm, reconfigure, and elaborate on the findings. In all three cases, other researchers could generate similar insights independently in other sites, on other occasions. Take, as an example, insights into the socially contextualized constitution of personal and community identity. Kondo's insights derive from personal experiences as a Japanese American in a relatively homogeneous culture. Leach's (1954) more macro insights in this general domain derive from his study of political systems in Highland Burma, a multiethnic field in which he was, unlike Kondo, not a partial insider. Other examples from the fields of "tribal" and ethnic studies could be offered (e.g., Haaland, 1969).

This contrast in method, yet convergence in the general nature of findings, illustrates the point made above that perspicacity is coupled only loosely with the details of the method. By contrast, details of thick descriptions are coupled rather tightly with the minutiae of procedure that led to their emergence. Clearly, no one but Kondo could have written about her experiences in company rituals. If we may provisionally extrapolate from the three examples covered, not only the details of description but the overall quality of a study is coupled rather tightly with the method. This appears plausible, at least in this sense, that the most fundamental tactics of method—site selection, time in the field, engaged participation with insiders, and intense consideration—establish the parameters of the caliber of the contribution that an ethnography can make. Malinowski may have been entirely on target after all: The ethnographer's magic really is the ethnographer's method.

APPENDIX
Editorial and Funding Review Checklist
for Ethnographic Method

Note: The questions that follow may be answered on the basis of either the method discussion or the body of the report.

A. Veracity

1. Prolonged Fieldwork

- Did the ethnographer spend long enough in the field? (This has customarily been construed as 12 to 18 months.) *Gouldner (1954): marginal (133-200 days at 7.5 hours per day), but used many observers, and effectively an insider participant (the labor relations director). Barker (1993): no (36.7 days at 7.5 hours per day)—a red flag, but Barker had previously been an insider in a self-managing team elsewhere. Kondo (1990): yes (26 months; more than a year as employee).*

- If not, was there at least episodic observation over a long period? Was there a reason for a shorter time spent in fieldwork, such as a specialized purpose (e.g., multiple-site efforts at theory disconfirmation)? Was there a reason that the site could be studied relatively quickly (e.g., prior knowledge of many aspects about the site)? *Gouldner (1954) and Barker (1993): both in own-language, own-culture sites apparently lacking in elaborate restricted codes. Kondo (1990): not applicable (n/a).*

- Does the study achieve "massive overdetermination of pattern (MOP)" (Agar, 1996)? *Gouldner (1954): not quite. Barker (1993): no. Kondo (1990): yes.*

- Did the ethnographer revisit the site? If so, at what intervals, and for what periods of time? What were the circumstances of the revisit(s)? For example, did the ethnographer make a "return" after publishing about the site in the interim? *Gouldner (1954): no. Barker (1993): no. Kondo (1990): made a 1-month visit to United States before returning to Japan in altered role.*

2. Seeking Out Reorienting or Disconfirming Observations

- Is there reason to think that the ethnographer actively sought out disconfirming and reorienting observations, and revised all assertions until all observations could be accounted for? *Gouldner (1954): apparently done in dialogue of research team. Barker (1993): some evidence for this, but questions remain; for example, the claim is made that "team members are relatively unaware of how the system they created actually controls their actions" (p. 434), but limited evidence is offered of effort to check up on this assertion with the full range of actors. Kondo (1990): evidence of considerable evolution of study, and of wide-ranging interviews.*

- Are the assertions and findings made sufficiently explicit that it would be (and would have been) possible to recognize disconfirming or reorienting observations? *Gouldner (1954): yes. Barker (1993): yes. Kondo (1990): less oriented to explicit assertions, but generally yes.*

3. Good Participative Role Relationships

- How well did the ethnographer's involvements in role relationships generate opportunities for unfettered inquiry? How well did they provide opportunities to witness? How well did they provide opportunities to experience? Did the ethnographer become the object of efforts at socialization into the culture of the site? *Gouldner (1954): unfettered, limited witnessing and experiencing (one student worked for one summer). Barker (1993): unfettered, but marginal witnessing and no experiencing. Kondo (1990): as Japanese American in Japan, utilized kinship roles in Japan and became object of socializing efforts.*

- Did the role involvements generate access to backstage interactions and performances? Did they lead to a wide, or to relatively skewed, range of perspectives and groupings that could be accessed? *Gouldner (1954): limited, comprehensive (modest skewing). Barker (1993): unlikely, unknown. Kondo (1990): yes to first question; intentionally skewed more to workers than to managers.*

- How actively did the ethnographer participate in role relationships at the site? Is the study based on Peripheral Member, Active

Member, or Complete Member Research (Adler & Adler, 1987)? *Gouldner (1954): generally PMR, but use of insider (CMR) and some AMR. Barker (1993): PMR only, but recall Barker's analogous experience elsewhere. Kondo (1990): generally AMR, verging on CMR.*

- How actively did insiders participate in the research process, on a continuum from passive objects of observation to (in some cases) professional colleagues? Did the study use opportunistic or native ethnography? *Gouldner (1954): very significantly as key informant (labor relations director spent at least one full month of work time). Barker (1993): no such participation, but insiders apparently were cooperative. Kondo (1990): verging on native ethnography.*

- What was the relationship between outsiders and insiders in the research process? At what stages of the process, from research design through write-up, were insiders involved? (To the extent that insiders were actively involved with an outsider in research, they should be considered along with the outsider ethnographer for answering the questions about participant observation.) *Gouldner (1954): unofficially a collaborative outsider-insider study. Barker (1993): scholar dominated. Kondo (1990): scholar dominated.*

- Is the ethnographer proficient in the language(s) of the actors? Does the ethnographer have skills (e.g., in crafts, medicine, business) required for active roles in participant observation? *Gouldner (1954): in language (miners' English) and mechanical skills. Barker (1993): familiarity with team-based management. Kondo (1990): good knowledge of Japanese language and customs.*

4. Attentiveness to Speech and Interactional Contexts

- Were speech and other activities observed in multiple contexts? Was speech-in-action recorded in multiple settings? *Gouldner (1954): yes but rather modestly; student team members did participate with workers after hours. Barker (1993): modestly; key informant and interview-based study; however, some key observations are from speech-in-action. Kondo (1990): yes.*

- Does the ethnographer clarify his or her own role in eliciting actors' utterances or other activities? Are any inhibiting or facilitating roles of other actors made apparent? Does the ethnographer demonstrate sensitivity to the contexts of activities that are reported? *Gouldner (1954): yes. Barker (1993): somewhat (given article length). Kondo (1990): ironically fairly unexplicit.*

- Were structured or unstructured dyadic or collective (focus group) interviews effectively used? Were variables-oriented interview methods employed? If so, are they appropriately documented? *Gouldner (1954): very extensive use of interviews. Barker (1993): extensive use of interviews. Kondo (1990): many interviews, but very little information given on their nature.*

5. Multiple Modes of Data Collection

- Does the ethnographer indicate the types of data collection used in the study? Is it apparent what types of data are used for different descriptive or analytic purposes? *Gouldner (1954): generally yes. Barker (1993): generally yes. Kondo (1990): generally yes.*

- Were a variety of data collection methods (including such possibilities as participant observation, interviews, insider documentation, outsider documentation, artifacts and photographs, surveys, and nonparticipative observation) employed? *Gouldner (1954): yes. Barker (1993): yes, a little more limited (interviews, observations; insider documents little used [?]). Kondo (1990): similar to Barker, but much more participant observation.*

- Was the data collection creative or resourceful? *Gouldner (1954): somewhat (students, insider, use of ex-soldiers' solidarity with employees). Barker (1993): very limited use of archival data. Kondo (1990): yes, regarding use of self as instrument.*

B. Objectivity

1. Trail of the Ethnographer's Path

- How fully does the report depict the researcher's realized pattern of interaction with the actors (the ethnographer's path), whether this depiction is by a reflexive writing style or in the method discussion? Is the "basic information on 'informants and contacts'" (Sanjek, 1990a) made available? *Gouldner (1954): vague. Barker (1993): vague. Kondo (1990): more forthcoming than Gouldner or Barker, but somewhat vague.*

- Does this information enable the reader to judge the extent and type of partisanship on the part of the author? Does it clarify the ethnographer's success in gaining the trust of multiple subgroupings? Does it reveal a deep and privileged access within at least some social units? *Gouldner (1954): (despite above) explicitly yes on all counts. Barker (1993): these remain questions about the study. Kondo (1990): yes on all counts.*

- Did the ethnographer actually observe a wide range of perspectives and subgroupings, so as to sample (so far as possible) the entire distribution of topics studied? *Gouldner (1954): yes. Barker (1993): observed each team and (somewhat) each shift; otherwise, not clear. Kondo (1990): yes, within framework of topical focus.*

2. Respondent Validation

- Were insiders offered the opportunity to comment on any of the ethnographer's draft reports? (Note that this is automatic in insider-outsider collaborative research.) *Gouldner (1954): apparently not. Barker (1993): apparently not. Kondo (1990): apparently not.*

- If there were such opportunities, were they used by insiders? How did the ethnographer use the feedback provided? *Gouldner (1954): n/a. Barker (1993): n/a. Kondo (1990): n/a.*

3. Feedback From Outsiders

- Assuming that the research was not team based, how did the ethnographer acquire and use feedback from other scholars during the process of research? *Gouldner (1954): team based, and (many) talks with scholarly colleagues. Barker (1993): talks with scholarly colleagues. Kondo (1990): very extensive scholarly feedback.*

4. Interrater Checks on Indexing and Coding

- Recall that interrater checks have serious limitations and modest benefits in ethnographic research.

- Did anyone, other than the ethnographer, check for Type I errors in the indexing and coding of the data? How did the other rater come to have the expertise required to do this? Note that checks for Type I errors (i.e., the most common form of interrater checks) have very serious limitations. *Gouldner (1954): used team discussions and outsider feedback extensively. Barker (1993): no, but did use outsider feedback. Kondo (1990): no, but did use outsider feedback.*

- Much more important, did anyone check for Type II errors in the indexing and coding of the data? Did someone, other than the ethnographer, independently index and code the data? If so, how different from the ethnographer, in experiences and perspectives, was this other person(s)? Recall that interrater checks are not the only means of such checks; others include saturating indexing and extensive searches on potentially related index words. *Gouldner (1954): as above. Barker (1993): no (data not apparently coded/indexed). Kondo (1990): no (data not apparently coded/indexed).*

- Was the entire record checked, or was it sampled? If it was sampled, how was this done? *Gouldner (1954): as above. Barker (1993): as above. Kondo (1990): as above.*

5. Comprehensive Data Archive

- Was the research team based, or was there a plan for the data record to be used by independent scholars? If these unusual conditions do not apply, this tactic is both unnecessary and unwise. *Gouldner (1954): team based with internal database. Barker (1993): n/a. Kondo (1990): n/a.*

C. Perspicacity

1. Intense Consideration of the Data

- Was there a self-disciplined process of data transformation that, in broad outline, included indexing and coding of the data, decontextualizing, memoing, and recontextualizing? (Other words, such as *search* and *retrieve,* are likely to be used.) For example, can it be determined how index words were prioritized and clustered in the creation of higher-order constructs? *Gouldner (1954): used extensive team discussions. Barker (1993): yes, like Gouldner using precomputer methods. Kondo (1990): implicitly, a noncomputerized tacit process.*

- Were a variety of other ethnographies and literatures used in the process of considering the data? *Gouldner (1954): yes. Barker (1993): yes. Kondo (1990): yes.*

2. Exploration

- Was the site chosen—before or after the fact—so as to promote exploration? For example, is the site interestingly unique, at an extreme of a theoretical spectrum, or full of wide internal variation? Does it enable either crucial case testing or the reinvestigation of earlier studies? *Gouldner (1954): use of comparisons of bureaucracy underground (in mine) and on surface, and of two types of regimes (due to managerial succession). Barker (1993): use of comparisons based on temporal developments in site that had recently developed self-managing teams. Kondo (1990): Japan an extreme site for highly socialized selves, company rituals (especially the "Ethics School") even more so; variations in Kondo's American experiences contrasted with Japanese experiences.*

- Was the ethnographer creative and persistent in seeking out potential points of contrast and reorientation, by means of maximizing the use of within-site variation? Most ethnographers do not search further afield, but was there an unusual use of documentary or library sources in this quest? Were other sites observed for this purpose? *Gouldner (1954): creative (as above). Barker (1993): good use of comparisons among three phases at site. Kondo (1990): creative in variation in her own experiences, less so with informants or actors.*

- Were comprehensive findings made available through any medium? *Gouldner (1954): not very comprehensive, but second book on strike at site was also published. Barker (1993): apparently not; very focused. Kondo (1990): more comprehensive than the other two, but still rather focused.*

NOTES

1. Whatever impact this book has will stem from two sources. The first is the debates that I hope this book will inspire. The second source is its stitching together of insights derived from other writers, such as Patricia and Peter Adler, Michael Agar, Howard Becker, Robert Emerson, Roger Sanjek, John Van Maanen, William Foote Whyte, and Harry Wolcott. Accordingly, I make an effort to mitigate my biases by drawing on a cosmopolitan set of literatures that is about one-quarter applied social research and a second quarter cultural anthropology, one-fifth social anthropology and a second fifth sociology, with the residual composed of other disciplines.

Although I cover multiple literatures, I do not try to cover all the factors that affect a reader's judgment of ethnographic quality. Neither do method discussions. Method discussions properly fail to cover the skills and interpretive crafts that produced that product (except those that directly enable observation—such as knowledge of the language—and participation—such as specialized skills), just as they avoid discussion of the quality of the ethnographic text (discussed by Adler & Adler, 1995; Leininger, 1994; Naroll, 1970a; Werner & Schoepfle, 1987, vol. 2, pp. 311-335).

Method discussions also need not make explicit the philosophical questions of ethics, epistemology, and ontology. This assertion about ethics has been debated in the literature. I would argue that ethics is not superordinate, but that ethics and method (uneasily) occupy equal space in ethnographic priorities. The central point is the irrelevance of moral rightness to method, *qua* method. One reason adduced by D'Andrade (1995), in his debate with Scheper-Hughes (1995), is that ethics, which is mute on the scientific merits of research, could make prescriptions for method only if the ethnographer compromises standards, developed for description or analysis, in order to advance his or her own views of goodness (see Harris's commentary in D'Andrade, 1995, and Scheper-Hughes, 1995).

2. Although I have no delusions about teasing the world into my own preferred consensus, I hope this book contributes to more consensus on method discussions. This applies to discussions not only in articles but also in books. I would hope to see at least more coverage. However, books have a length that supports many ways of reporting on method, and reviewers of book manuscripts are astute consumers of ethnography. Articles require more concise, hence standardized, coverage. Thus, I focus on discussions in articles more than in books.

3. See Emerson, Fretz, and Shaw (1995, pp. 201-204), Stocking (1992, p. 13), and Wolcott (1994, p. 398).

4. For nonanthropologists: This reference is to Miner's (1956) classic amusement on Nacirema (American) culture; an application of the concept to academic publishing is found in Stewart (1995).

5. See Fine (1993), Hammersley (1990, p. 131), Nader (1976), Smith (1984), and Yin (1984, p. 56).

6. See also Janesick (1994), Rosen (1991), and Sutton (1997). Geertz (1990) is convinced that a book such as this is bound to be "largely bootless" (p. 324).

7. See also Agar (1986b, p. 53), Sanjek (1991), Silverman (1993, p. 153), and Wolcott (1994, pp. 19, 350).

8. See Agar (1986b, 1996, p. 37), Gliner (1994), Markus (1992), Muecke (1994), Sanjek (1991), Schofield (1990), Sutton (1997), and Wolcott (1990a, 1994, pp. 27, 37).

9. For discussion of naturalistic involvement, see Adler and Adler (1987), Agar (1986b), Hammersley (1990, p. 1), Wolcott (1992), and Van Maanen (1988, pp. 3, 9); for exploration with actors and insiders, see Agar (1986b), Barth (1995), Bloch (1991); Jenkins (1994), Rabinow (1977), and Riemer (1977).

10. Calls to comprehensiveness are found in the work of Malinowski (1922/1961, p. 11), Lutkehaus (1990), and Sanjek (1990b). Ethnographers are not the omniscient beings that Rabinow (1977, p. 3) sees as implied by the range of coverage in traditional ethnographies. (Compare the classic guides to comprehensiveness—Murdock et al., 1987; Royal Anthropological Institute, 1951—with the plea for "naive" limitations on interdisciplinarity in Devons & Gluckman, 1964.) In Rabinow's (1977) view, anthropologists have perhaps been more successful at observing situations, such as rituals, in which "boundaries are easily discernable," than they have at observing "day-to-day activity and common-sense reasoning" (p. 58; but compare Bloch, 1991; Jenkins, 1994).

11. See also Van Maanen (1988, p. 22), Agar (1986b, p. 29), Frayser (1996), and Wolcott (1994, p. 160). Abbott (1997) provides an explication of spatial and temporal contextualisms in the context of Chicago school sociology, and their absence in the rest, that is, in variables-oriented sociology.

12. The word *culture* may have unfortunate connotations. Barth (1995) has argued that the "prototype" of "culture" as "an assemblage of *customs* as an integrated, locally shared way of life" (p. 66) has three baneful consequences: exoticizing the "other," depersonalizing the "other," and encouraging ethnic political entrepreneurship. Moreover, applied researchers have little to gain by declaring in favor of either view, but ought not to stress culture at the expense of social relations. For example, in management ethnography, much of the topical emphasis is on social relations and activities, such as work flows and economic transactions. In these domains (as in many others), actual behaviors may well be at odds with cultural norms (Barth, 1989).

13. See also Agar (1986b), Geertz (1976), Van Maanen (1988, p. 50), Wikan (1991), and Wolcott (1994, p. 167).

14. Glaser and Strauss (1967) draw a distinction between grounded theory and ethnography: The grounded theoretical sociologist "is an active sampler of theoretically relevant data, not an ethnographer trying to get the fullest data on a group" (p. 58; compare p. 35). Still, this earlier book is closer to the spirit of ethnography than Strauss's later works, such as Strauss (1987) and Strauss and Corbin (1990) (see Stern, 1994).

15. For discussion of contextually grounded thinking, see Agar (1986b, p. 32), Boyle (1994), Lofland (1995), and Muecke (1994).

16. See Boyle (1994), Leininger (1994), Wolcott (1994), and Yin (1984, p. 14).

17. They added a fifth criterion for purposes of dealing with false information from informants. To me, this is an aspect of veracity or their "credibility." (Gliner's [1994] adaptation for ethnography is implicit.)

18. Stepwise replication involves the use of "two separate research teams . . . [that] deal separately with data sources that have been cut into halves" (Guba, 1981, p. 87). Lincoln and Guba (1985) abandoned this procedure as "very cumbersome" (p. 317). Guba's earlier advocacy of the approach remains instructive, because stepwise replication runs counter to the values ethnographers place on holism and contextualism (as well as emergent learning, as Lincoln & Guba, 1985, observe). I discuss and generally dismiss the use of audit trails in ethnography in Chapter 4. Another clue that naturalistic inquiry is not the same as ethnography is that there are only two ethnographic or anthropological works in Guba's (1981) reference list.

Lincoln and Guba (1985, chap. 11) add two tactics to those noted by Guba (1981). One, a "reflexive journal" (p. 327), can be subsumed under the ethnographer's path as a helpful but not essential device (Ottenberg, 1990). The other, "negative case analysis" (pp. 309-313), is very similar to seeking out reorienting or disconfirming observations.

19. See also Hammersley (1990, p. 54), LeCompte and Preissle (1993, p. 323), and Stocking (1992, p. 330). Of course, one purpose of the Qualitative Research Method Series is to remedy this problem.

20. See Comaroff and Comaroff (1992, chap. 1) and Hunt (1991, p. 384) for a similar point about natural scientists; see generally D'Andrade (1995) and Searle (1995, chap. 9).

21. Antiscience arguments are strongest (and, I suspect, most widely believed) when they focus on epistemological limitations, such as the purportedly inevitable theory-ladenness of observation. This argument, if valid, would render impossible the objective testing of theory. The (limited) validity and general weakness of this argument is clearly addressed by Hunt (1994). Along the same (preemptive strike) lines, I find it curious how many social scientists casually take it as a well-known—I almost said "fact"—whatever-they-consider-what-is-well-known that philosophical concepts such as reality, truth, foundationalism, and modernism are obsolete. The likelihood of these concepts simply withering away is on the face of it implausible. Moreover, concepts like these have a fecund capacity to mutate, and devastating attacks upon them generally turn out to be directed at the weakest of the strains.

22. It follows that replication is impossible. Now, there are those who argue the contrary, but they have not convinced me that they refer to ethnography. White (1990) asserts that reliability can be measured for all aspects of ethnography, but so far as one can see he applies reliability only to cross-cultural coding and scale construction. Johnson (1990, pp. 15-20) apparently would prefer to argue in favor of replication, but concedes that "replication, in the strictest sense" (p. 19) is impossible.

23. As Kirk and Miller (1986, p. 10) note, objectivity has various meanings. They treat objectivity as subsuming both validity and reliability (pp. 13, 19-20), and hold that the essential aspect for qualitative researchers is the willingness "to take an intellectual risk—the risk of being demonstrably [i.e., empirically] wrong" (p. 10; see also Hunt, 1994). This latter sense is the core one in my use of the word *objectivity* in this book. Megill (1994) distinguishes four "senses of objectivity," three of which apply here. Obviously applicable is "procedural" objectivity, which finds the locus of objectivity in proper adherence to canons of method (pp. 10-11). Perhaps "disciplinary objectivity" is equally applicable, for its emphasis on the community of inquirers, or "the proximate convergence of accredited inquirers within a given field" (p. 5). "Dialectical [objectivity], which holds that objects are constituted *as* objects in the course of interplay between subject and object" (pp. 1, 7-10), is also applicable to ethnography (Fabian, 1991).

24. The layout and rationale of Table 2.1 are borrowed from Guba (1981). Standards are the expectations about the extent to which research method tactics have been used so as to approximate research values. Thus, references to the tactics as *criteria* are contractions. *Expectations* is the term used to subsume both criteria and method. In Cicchetti (1991), what I am calling goals and tactics are "attributes," and "criteria" are norms used to judge performance regarding attributes.

25. Brinberg and McGrath (1985) argue that research designs can maximize "precision," "generalizability," or "realism," but one, and only one, of these values. They also argue that field studies succeed best in achieving "realism of context," but "have relatively little precision with respect to measurement and control of variables because [the re-

searcher] will not want to be intrusive [i.e., there is little control over consistency] . . . and [these studies] will have relatively little generalizability to populations beyond the specific setting" (p. 43; see also Asad, 1994).

26. See, for example, Johnson and Johnson (1990), Kirk and Miller (1986), and Sanjek (1990a). Compare Altheide and Johnson (1994) and Lincoln and Denzin (1994). See generally Babbie (1983, pp. 118-119).

27. In qualitative research, cases that do not fit the argument are not, as in conventional research, assumed to be inevitable "error" amenable to statistical controls, but rather to be cause for revision of the argument (Katz, 1983; Ragin, 1987). However, a goal of zero error should not be taken to mean that no mistakes are made.

28. Much of Bowlin and Stromberg's (1997) argument is predicated on their unsubstantiated assertion that "what scientific realists assume [is] that true beliefs are nothing but the accurate representation of the world in the mind" (p. 124; compare Chapter 2 of this volume and Hunt, 1991, p. 380). Otherwise, most of their argument is consistent with mine.

29. See, for example, Bernard (1994), Chagnon (1968), Dean and Whyte (1958), Nachman (1984), Shulman (1994), and Wallendorf and Belk (1989). Nachman (1984) makes several cautionary observations. He notes that the customary ethnographic practice of asking everyone the same question may make the inquirer seem untrustworthy. So also might the ethnographer's tendency not to say what is believed in the actors' culture. Moreover, the most articulate actors may, for that reason, be both the best informants and the most accomplished liars. John Van Maanen, fiendishly, caught an irony here: If this is so, how could my readers trust me as an informant on ethnography?

An illustration of Nachman's conundrums (source: my former professor, P. H. Gulliver) also illustrates the stories used to teach method in social anthropology. Richards was in her tent, listening through the canvas as her "native" (I don't recall if this word was used) paid assistant regaled his companions with tale after tale about his experiences of her. All of these tales homed in, for their moral, on her serious cognitive deficiencies. For example, she was never able to understand what she was told at only one hearing; she always asked the same simple, perfectly obvious question of everybody she met. Couldn't she ever remember what she'd been told? Eventually, the local raconteur paused to compose himself sufficiently as to exonerate his employer. "Well, you do have to admit," he allowed, "that *at least she's fat.*" As it happens, she wasn't fat; his meaning was that she was well-to-do. This story also points to an objectivity-enhancing tactic that is seldom used any longer—the paid field assistant: "I cannot overrate the importance of my assistant in this research, for he acted as an important check on my observations and I on his" (Kapferer, 1972, p. xx).

30. See Agar (1996, pp. 32-33), Rosen (1991), and Whyte (1984, p. 47).

31. See Emerson (1987), Naroll (1970a), Ottenberg (1994), and Stoller (1994).

32. These are called "rich points" in Agar (1996, pp. 31-34) and "new experiences" in Rudie (1994).

33. See Firth (1977), Garbett (1967), Mayer (1989), Ottenberg (1994), and Wolcott (1994, p. 350).

34. See Foster, Scudder, Colson, and Kemper (1979), Garbett (1967), and Kirchgassler (1991).

35. See Davis (1993), Ellis (1995), Mahmood and Armstrong (1992), and Ottenberg (1987).

36. The contribution of a restudy, by which I mean a later study of (pretty much) the same site by another researcher, is harder to evaluate. Some authors have seen the restudy as clearly useful only for veracity (actually, validity; see Sanjek, 1990a: "It was *validity*

that they [Lewis contra Redfield and Freeman contra Mead] challenged"; p. 394); others have seen it as useful for reliability (Naroll, 1970a: "Restudies . . . are studies of reliability . . . of consistency, not of accuracy"; p. 931). It appears that restudies would commingle issues of veracity (for example, Were the role relationships adequate?), consistency (What differences in findings are due to changes in the site?), and perspicacity (Which researcher's analysis penetrates to the heart of the issues? What contingencies affect the application elsewhere?). As is so often the case, terminology in this area is clouded. Garbett's (1967) *restudy* is what Mayer (1989) and I call a *revisit.* Mayer distinguishes a *multiple visit study* from a *revisit,* reserving the latter term for inquiries directed at social change and continuity. *Returns* is a term for restudies that follow publication of results of earlier visits (Davis, 1993; Ellis, 1995).

37. See also Becker and Geer (1960), Dreher (1994), Katz (1983), and Silverman (1993, p. 162).

38. Another way to say this is that they need data of the sort enabled by tactics like restudies and an extensive ethnographer's path (see Chapter 4). The qualities of these data are construed by Bailyn (1977) in terms of data complexity and surplus; by Campbell (1975) and by March, Sproull, and Tamuz (1991) in terms of multiple observations and implications; by Kidder (1981) in terms of maximizing the different methods of measurement; and by Werner and Schoepfle (1987, vol. 1) in terms of distinctions made in the record (such as those distinguishing the observer's views, actors' statements, and conditions of statements). With such data, one could find, to give two examples, that an incident occurred at a different time relative to another than one would expect, or that a belief is expressed by an unexpected category of actors. A way to express this for organizations studies scholars is that ethnographers are ultracontingency theorists.

Rosenblatt (1981, p. 198) appears to hold that the search for negative instances can occur in the field only if the purpose is to be "theory probing," and that postfieldwork searches of this type are "only illustrative." This appears to be wrong because it fails to recognize both the complexity of ethnographic data (which makes them impossible to remember in their entirety) and the multifaceted character of these data.

39. See Agar (1996, p. 16), Louis and Bartunek (1992), Rabinow (1977), Tedlock (1991), and Whyte (1984, pp. 74, 223). Ethnography is a participation-based mode of inquiry that does not privilege the "outsider" as uniquely occupying "the domain of objectivity," construed in "unbridgeable opposition" to the "subjectivity" of the insider (Tedlock, 1991, p. 71).

40. Just as the nonparticipative observer is not an ethnographic role for outsiders, so too the passive object of inquiry is not an ethnographic role for insiders. However, ethnographic studies include observations of such insiders because (except in the smallest-scale studies) not all insiders can or wish to be involved.

41. The former model is so much more the tradition in academic social science that the latter model might seem hypothetical. However, that model is well established in applied social research, as in cases in which internal organizational change consultants may hire in external help for their projects. That model might also become more common in academic research (Agar, 1996, pp. 11, 16-23).

42. Lave and Wenger (1991) conceptualize the locus of cognition not in self-contained information that can be decontextualized and transported across actors' minds, but in processes of coparticipation embedded in interactional contexts.

43. See Dalton (1967), Rosen (1991), Van Maanen (1983), and Whyte (1984, p. 30).

44. The concept of "the ethnographer's path" (Sanjek, 1990a; see also Chapter 4) refers to the researcher's realized pattern of interaction with actors. The concept of the

ethnographer's roles refers to social spaces that are occupied as these create both the potential and constraints for such paths.

45. See also Agar (1986b, pp. 38-39), Barth (1989), Becker and Geer (1960), Emerson et al. (1995, p. 140), Gluckman (1961), Whyte (1984, p. 69), and Wolcott (1994, p. 348).

46. For coding existing studies, see Stewart, Learned, Mandel, and Peterson (1995); for statistics-oriented interviewing, see Aunger (1994), Brim and Spain (1974, p. 22), and White (1990). The major limitation of Aunger's (1994) approach is that, because it is based on holding context constant, it is not suited to participant observation. It is challenging enough to do as he has done, which is to get different interviewers to ask the same respondents the same questions. Getting ethnographers to act as clones for one another, and also getting actors to indulge them in this, is inconceivable. His approach does not work for recording speech-in-action or anything else actors naturally *do.* (See generally Layder's and Sangren's commentaries in Aunger, 1995.)

47. The capacity of the interview, whether dyadic or group, to elicit discussion of virtually any desired topic (assuming rapport has been achieved) is the reason it has advantages over participant observation for the exploration of feelings and cognitions (Kleinman, Stenross, & McMahon, 1994; Morgan, 1988, p. 17). However, the theories of culture presented by anthropologists such as Barth (discussed above) imply that there are limitations in any explicit interviews or even speech-in-action on those topics.

48. The list of types of data is adapted from Yin (1984, pp. 79-89), who distinguishes documents from archives and disassociates surveys from "case study" research. An important but unusual type of document produced by insiders consists of responses to research reports (called *respondent validation* below). In rare and difficult circumstances, the documents produced by outsiders include other ethnographers' field notes (Lutkehaus, 1990; Smith, 1990; Stewart et al., 1995). With survey data, one should distinguish attribute data (e.g., age and opinions) from relational data (i.e., social network ties). Both may be useful. For discussion of triangulation in ethnography, see Guba (1981), Hammersley (1990, p. 84), Kirk and Miller (1986, p. 30), Kritzer (1994), and Werner and Schoepfle (1987, vol. 1).

49. See Johnson (1990), Kirk and Miller (1986, pp. 50-52), Leonard-Barton (1990), and Lyon (1997).

50. See Ervin-Tripp (1996), Keane (1997), Kondo (1990, chaps. 5-6), Lave and Wenger (1991), and Parmentier (1994, pp. 68-69).

51. See, for example, Bolyanatz (1995a), Sahlins (1961), Schlegel (1972), and Strathern (1987).

52. See also Adler and Adler (1987, pp. 56, 63), Elsworth (1994), Lofland (1995), Scheper-Hughes (1995), and Van Maanen (1983).

53. See, for example, Altheide and Johnson (1994), Aunger (1995), Brewer (1994), Dreher (1994), and Silverman (1993, pp. 145-149).

54. See also Frayser (1996), Stocking (1992), Werner and Schoepfle (1987, vol. 1, pp. 62-63), and Wolcott (1994, p. 159).

55. The potential for interaction that is afforded by the roles, and the capacities, as opportunities for experience, both affect veracity, for reasons presented in Chapter 3. For reasons presented in this chapter, the potential for interaction also affects objectivity, as does the capacity adopted (e.g., part-time laborer, student, apprentice, anthropologist), because it powerfully colors perspective, even if it need not cause outright partisanship.

56. Admittedly, this logic sets in play an illogically infinite loop because it would call for reporting also the social networks of these informants' key informants, and theirs, and theirs . . . .

57. There are some exceptions where the informant's abilities should be noted. Reasons for the advantages (e.g., access to secret documents, extensive travels) and disadvantages (e.g., bitter partisanship, memory lapses) of working with particular key informants should be noted, if these could materially affect any claims.

58. An effective field-worker will learn things that cannot be repeated, without violating the informal contract according to which confidences were revealed (Adler & Adler, 1993). The ethnographer's path, when it succeeds in method terms, by penetrating the insiders' "dirt" (aggressive metaphor), may raise ethical questions. If the insiders' secrets are revealed in such a way that could be deciphered (even if only by insiders), the reader should ask whether or not there was any misleading of the actors about the researcher's true goals, or even if there was subterfuge on the part of the field-worker (Becker, 1970, p. 113; Ellis, 1995; Punch, 1986).

A second method-ethics conflict afflicts the reporting of the ethnographer's path. Because of the possibility that reports will be read by the actors, and the near inevitability of differences of interests among them, the identities of key informants may have to be hidden, or at least well disguised.

59. From an epistemic perspective, both the insiders and outsiders will bring a relatively homogeneous set of biases to their reading, and it is hard to get real cultural outsiders, who would be needed for reducing error through comparison of multiple biases, to examine the study (LeVine, 1981).

60. My guess is that few such arcs—pardon me, arcs are directed lines or ties or connections—would merit reporting. The main exceptions would be those in research teams and those between doctoral students and their advisers, although even these ties may be fairly weak, due to independence derived from lengthy periods off in the field.

61. Intrarater agreement indicates consistency. As in Miles and Huberman's (1994) standards, percentages of agreement are commonly reported indicators. For more sophisticated, but also imperfect, measures, see Brennan and Hays (1992), who recommend the use of both percentage agreement and the kappa statistic.

62. Ethnographers can, as noted, incorporate nonethnographic methods, and can quantify ethnographic data for purposes of mathematical data transformation (Behrens, 1990). One ought not underestimate "the measurement potential of ethnographic field-notes" (Johnson & Johnson, 1990). I personally have an interest in using ethnographic data for the creation of social network data that are amenable to quantitative analysis (Sayles & Stewart, 1995; Stewart & Krackhardt, 1997). However, one also should not underestimate the differences between statistical research and ethnography (well articulated by Asad, 1994; Ragin, 1987; Seidel, Kjolseth, & Seymour, 1988, pp. 7-1, 7-8). For that reason, as well as the topical focus of this book, the treatment of method for data consideration, below, refers only to textual data.

63. The emergent and iterative character of ethnographic data consideration means there is no reason not to iron out virtually all disagreements among raters, and make the proud but hollow claim of 100% or near-100% agreement.

64. In conventional research, the appearance is that all raters equivalently execute a coding system, but this system itself was created by the researcher, who is for this reason not equivalent to (mere) "raters." From a design perspective, the researcher is not a rater but a coder, and the only coder. To be accurate, Kirk and Miller (1986) should be credited

with also reporting on "'Type three error' [which] is asking the wrong questions" (pp. 29-30). This is an important source of error, but not one amenable to methodological correction.

65. I have found it easier to satisfy this requirement by selecting from a pool of research assistants not closely affiliated with me (the researcher), whereas the task of checking for Type I errors falls to one or more of "my own" graduate students. Academic ethnographers may find my experience fairly typical. Regardless of selection of raters, checking for both Type I and Type II errors could be accomplished through random sampling of the data.

66. See Guba (1981), Huberman and Miles (1983), Rodgers and Cowles (1993), Schwandt and Halpern (1988), Wallendorf and Belk (1989), and Yin (1984, pp. 92-96). In grounded theory, not only must the data be written, so must all of the analysis. As Muecke (1994) argues, "In contrast to the standards of grounded theory, neither rigor in documentation nor auditability of decision-making trails [is] required of an ethnography" (p. 204).

67. See Fox (1994), Goodstein (1991), Hammersley (1997), and Wallendorf and Belk (1989).

68. See also Hammersley (1997), Kritzer (1994), Malinowski (1922/1961, pp. 3-4), Ottenberg (1990), Plath (1990), and Van Maanen (1988, pp. 123-124).

69. Lab scientists do not report the 19 failed efforts prior to the successful running of an assay. Although their lab notes include all recorded data, failed assays do not produce data.

70. Another liability to audit trails and their requisite archives is less apparent, unless one is a lawyer, as Akeroyd is. She points to the complications that would arise from data protection legislation, arguing that legal measures intended to protect against harm caused by governmental or commercial databases can also be applied to social scientists. The implication is that researchers must be cautious, *especially* if they use machine-readable data, to ensure that data are securely held and, in case security were to be breached, that actors are not identifiable (Akeroyd, 1991). This is a nice—no, a perverse example of the unforeseen effects of policies designed with the purest of purposes.

71. See Becker (1990), Hammersley (1990, pp. 97-102), Kidder (1981), and Yin (1984, pp. 36, 39).

72. See Fox (1967, pp. 111-114), Richards (1950, pp. 246-251), and Schlegel (1972, pp. 3-4).

73. See Bolyanatz (1995a, 1995b), Leach (1961), Schneider (1961), and Watson-Franke (1992, 1995). A very quick take on Leach (1961, chap. 1) is that kinship has no explanatory power. For a nuanced discussion, see Schlegel (1972, pp. 136-141). At the opposite end of the spectrum from Leach's nominalism is Watson-Franke's descent-determinism (ably countered by Bolyanatz, 1995a). Watson-Franke (1992) argues that a non-Western, feminist understanding of the matrilineal male "philosophy" would reveal that "the matrilineal puzzle dissolves" (p. 486). Bolyanatz (1995a, 1995b) points to Watson-Franke's impressionistic (very well, tendentious) use of evidence (as she does in kind for him), but unfortunately he accedes to her psychologizing away of the social structural basis of the puzzle. This basis (contrary to her reframing) is *not* focused on the male's tensions between ties to his household versus ties to his descent group (that is, his roles as father and husband versus his roles—the roles involving control over inheritable assets—as brother). Watson-Franke was influenced by Schneider (1961, pp. 13-14), who refers to psychological strains, but also the structural strains that are the focus of

Richards's thesis. Even if Watson-Franke were convincing that one ought to reject the construct of the matrilineal puzzle (and doubtless she has convinced to some), this would still serve as an example of perspicacity. A perspicacious construct, like all empirical constructs, ought to be amenable to reconstruction and disconfirmation.

74. For (secondhand) biology, see McKelvey (1982); for social science, see Mandel (1996), Miller and Friesen (1984, pp. 3, 7), Stewart (1995), and Ulrich and McKelvey (1990).

75. Mandel (1996) notes that polythetism makes classification easier in this sense, that "not all clustering components must be similar." However, to give a sense of the problem, he also "found that 22.6% of the organizations sampled could be reclassified on the basis of imprecise criteria of polythetic classification" (p. 127). Moreover, there is another problem. In human worlds polythetism leads to a proliferation of taxa. Taxa the social scientist seeks to define are doubly polythetic—not only in terms of their objectively registered features, but also in terms of human definitions, which, furthermore, are heterogeneously dispersed among actors, any one of whom may impute categories on the basis of multiple, independently operating criteria (Needham, 1975, p. 364).

This problem is recognized, and conceptualized somewhat differently, in comparative political science. My colleagues and I have borrowed the language of Sartori (1970) and Collier and Mahon (1993) to argue that "it is not a given that concepts grounded in one field can 'travel' to other fields, without being 'stretched' to the point of distortion" (Stewart et al., 1995, p. 179). These latter comparativists refer not to monothetic but to "classical" categories, not to polythetic but to "radial" categories (Stewart et al., 1995, pp. 180-181). Classical categories increase in "extension" (generalization) as they decrease in "intension" (the number of defining attributes). Classical categories, if you will, survive intension by having a thick conceptual core. Thus, they travel well, and folk typologies that refer to classical realities may not be too much off the mark. However, many categories are empirically radial. Radial categories increase in extension by increasing in intension. For example, one may need to refer not to (classically construed) "entrepreneurship," but to categories like (as a guess) "lineage-based South Chinese trading companies" (Stewart et al., 1995, p. 181; see generally Collier & Mahon, 1993, fig. 2). There are thus two difficulties. One is the tendency to think in classical terms about radial realities. The other is that, absent substantiated empirical taxonomies, extension in a radial world is invalid.

76. This style of research has been exemplified above by Schlegel (1972). Ember (1997) offers an overview and prospectus; other commentaries may be found in Barnes (1971, chap. 1), Frayser (1996), Moran (1995), and Stewart et al. (1995, pp. 176-177).

77. Although HRAF research has tended, thus far, to be synchronic, "the HRAF Collection of Archaeology" is a newly developing effort to create "time series data" for diachronic analysis (Ember, 1997, p. 11).

78. For a good conceptual start to the range of temporal "dimensions" that need to be considered ("continuity, magnitude, rate of change, trend, periodicity, and . . . duration"), see Monge (1990). Heise (1991) and his colleagues have made a start at using ethnographic data for process analysis, using his event structure analytic approach. Morse (1998) also uses this approach in modeling Learned's (1995) ethnographic data.

To my mind, the failure of the extended case studies (for example, Gulliver, 1971; Kapferer, 1972; Oppong, 1974; Turner, 1957; Van Velsen, 1964) to live up to their long-term promise, which was extremely high, stems not from their quality, which is certainly high, but from the failure of others to systematize the results. These studies traded off the number of actors and places observed in favor of depth of observation of a small number of actors (Van Velsen, 1967). Their impact would thus be severely limited if the only apparent findings were the interactional details (many of them dealing with actors' creative manipulations of norms and uses of resources from different arenas to advance their interests over time; see Stewart, 1990). These studies do include useful fodder for correlational comparisons; for example, Van Velsen (1964, p. 316) suggests that those actors who learn to navigate the complex and flexible negotiations of matrilineal systems (also Douglas, 1969; Oppong, 1974) develop interpersonal skills that effect disproportionate representation among the elite. However, the processual focus of these studies should also have enabled the analysis of temporal patterns.

79. There is a temptation to overuse the word *comparison* and to use Glaser and Strauss's (1967) expression "constant comparison" as a stock phrase to represent the entire process of considering the data. The temptation stems from ethnography's want of a handy phrase of its own, *decontextualize* and *recontextualize* being improbable candidates. Comparisons *are* centrally important, particularly for answering questions related to the applicability of an idea or pattern found elsewhere to explain the site, and vice versa. However, the mental process involved is not restricted to comparison. Data consideration in ethnography includes other mental activities, including getting materials ordered in a temporal sequence and forming a narrative; noticing and labeling; bundling, categorizing, and recategorizing; guesswork, intuition, and metaphorical inference; analysis, logic, and synthesis; and pattern seeking, modeling, and theory building. It would be stretching the word *comparison* to include all these activities. I use a more generic term, *consider,* to indicate this wider range of mental processes.

80. There is great value in a close reading and coding of field notes. This value is not a function of the sophistication of that technology, nor is the value of computer retrievals superior due to their relative sophistication. Nevertheless, Emerson et al. (1995) un- derestimate the value of computerized decontextualization and recontextualization. These processes enable a mode of concept development that is more suited to ethnography than the grounded theory-influenced model of dimensionalizing that they occasionally adopt (see, e.g., p. 149). Below, I refer to an ethnographic alternative to grounded theorizing that is consistent with their approach in terms of "orders" (e.g., second order) of indexing.

81. This is Becker and Geer's (1960, p. 281) principal of "full coding." Richards and Richards (1994, p. 454), creators of the rival NUD•IST software package, take the Ethnograph package to task on three grounds. Without suggesting that the Ethnograph is superior, let alone ideal, one could take issue with them, because it is a violation of the principal of objectivity for particular package creators to have written the chapter on software in the *Handbook of Qualitative Research.*

Their first assertion is the alleged loss of context. It appears that they simply misunderstand both Seidel's terminology and the Ethnograph's capacities on this score. Second, they say that the Ethnograph creates problems in "constructing new categories after the coding of many records without those categories" (p. 454). The Ethnograph has glitches in this regard, but there are no major problems. Their third assertion is that the Ethnograph forces research into more discreet phases of fieldwork—indexing, analysis, and so on. There is no reason that this package need do this more than any others.

82. Morse (1994) emphasizes the *theoretical* dimension of recontextualization, on the grounds that theory can be generalized to other sites, but here Richards and Richards (1994) appear correct in asserting that the new context that is based on decontextualization may be either factual or conceptual, or both.

83. Some of these files of second-order constructs would be more abstract; most, likely, would be more prosaic. Careful rearrangements of these files, like the slips of bamboo in ancient Chinese manuscripts, could constitute an opening draft of an ethnographic report. Whyte (1984) asserts that this result can be obtained by arrangements of first-order searches. "In writing a report," he notes, "we can work directly from the index to the outline of the paper" (p. 118). Most likely, he refers really to second-order searches, or elides the tacit steps that he must have used to produce *Street Corner Society* (1993) and *Human Relations in the Restaurant Industry* (1948).

84. See Agar (1991), Asad (1994), Whyte (1984, p. 21), and Wolcott (1994, pp. 24, 258).

85. In earlier drafts, I called this first tactic *disciplined techniques of data transformation*. Ethnographers writing for those who place little value on the insight aspect of perspicacity might do well to emphasize the disciplined and rigorous aspects of data transformation.

86. As Johnson and Johnson (1990) contend, because words in a data set have multiple meanings, a count of their occurrences would be meaningless. However, this does not apply to index words. As Kidder (1981, p. 246) implies, counts of index words, also, would not reflect distributions in a population, but they would count the number of times a particular *content* was observed, and in this sense (a consistency sense) provide a kind of "reliability check." The incidence of various index words can be quite revealing of the observer's presence (or lack thereof) in backstage performances. Access to the insider's perspective, an issue of veracity, can therefore be inferred from such incidence figures.

87. See Adler and Adler (1995), Barth (1989), Rosen (1991), and Stewart (1990).

88. See Dalton (1967), Hayano, (1979), Learned and Stewart (1994), and Riemer (1977).

89. Perhaps the simplest way to express Eckstein's (1975/1992) argument is to use his analogy of a theory as represented by a (bell or other) curve, which "only represents the principles . . . that give rise to empirically discerned curves" (p. 153). One could make no inferences about support or nonsupport of the theory on the basis of any single sampled observation—even assuming one could determine it lay somewhere on the curve—if (as in random sampling) one did not know where the point lies on the curve. However, ruleful theory would specify whether or not one has a case that is modal, or most likely to fit, and whether or not one has a case that is an outlier, or least likely to fit the theory. If the former observation does not conform to the theory, or if the latter does, the theory is disconfirmed.

90. See especially LeVine (1981, pp. 186-187); also Brim and Spain (1974, pp. 82-84) and Katz (1983).

91. Examples of matched comparisons include Dore (1973) and Wiewel and Hunter (1985); see also Eckstein (1975/1992, p. 118). For case replication research, see Leonard-Barton (1990) and Eckstein (1975/1992, pp. 143-147), who use the term *heuristic case studies*. Other advocates of multiple-site research include Huberman and Miles (1983), Lyon (1997), Stewart (1990), Whyte (1984, p. 140), and Yin (1984, pp. 39-40).

92. See, for example, Brewer (1994), Guba (1981), Leininger (1994), Schofield (1990), and Werner and Schoepfle (1987, vol. 2, p. 312).

93. It might appear odd to praise Kondo's *Crafting Selves* (1990) for its objectivity, as it might not seem to aspire to such a value. Moreover, Kondo does not attend as well as Gouldner (say) to some objectivity-enhancing tactics. However, Kondo does use a language (so awkward but so inevitable in ethnography) of "most," "many," "by my poll," and so on. She makes a concerted effort to depict the historical context. She also interacts with a great many actors, and renders herself vulnerable to others' definitions of the

situation; that is, moreover, the foundation of her findings. Hers is the most rhetorically experimental of the works, but (as the checklist demonstrates) fundamentally the most classically ethnographic. Due to her book's postmodern orientation (see, for example, pp. 17, 42, 47), I wish to state for the record that I regard it as splendid.

REFERENCES

Abbott, A. (1992). From causes to events: Notes on narrative positivism. *Sociological Methods & Research, 20,* 428-455.

Abbott, A. (1997). Of time and space: The contemporary relevance of the Chicago school. *Social Forces, 75,* 1149-1182.

Adler, P. A., & Adler, P. (1987). *Membership roles in field research.* Newbury Park, CA: Sage.

Adler, P. A., & Adler, P. (1993). Ethical issues in self-censorship. In C. M. Renzetti & R. M. Lee (Eds.), *Researching sensitive topics* (pp. 249-266). Newbury Park, CA: Sage.

Adler, P. A., & Adler, P. (1995). The demography of ethnography. *Journal of Contemporary Ethnography, 24,* 3-29.

Agar, M. H. (1986a). *Independents declared: The dilemmas of independent trucking.* Washington, DC: Smithsonian Institution Press.

Agar, M. H. (1986b). *Speaking of ethnography.* Beverly Hills, CA: Sage.

Agar, M. H. (1991). The right brain strikes back. In N. G. Fielding & R. M. Lee (Eds.), *Using computers in qualitative research* (pp. 181-194). London: Sage.

Agar, M. H. (1996). *The professional stranger* (2nd ed.). San Diego, CA: Academic Press.

Akeroyd, A. V. (1991). Personal information and qualitative research data: Some practical and ethical problems arising from data protection legislation. In N. G. Fielding & R. M. Lee (Eds.), *Using computers in qualitative research* (pp. 89-106). London: Sage.

Aldrich, H. E., Fowler, S. W., Liou, N., & Marsh, S. J. (1994). Other people's concepts: Why and how we sustain historical continuity in our field. *Organization, 1,* 65-80.

Altheide, D. L., & Johnson, J. M. (1994). Criteria for assessing interpretive validity in qualitative research. In N. K. Denzin & Y. S. Lincoln (Eds.), *Handbook of qualitative research* (pp. 485-499). Thousand Oaks, CA: Sage.

American Psychological Association. (1994). *Publication manual of the American Psychological Association* (4th ed.). Washington, DC: Author.

Asad, T. (1994). Ethnographic representation, statistics and modern power. *Social Research, 61,* 55-88.

Aunger, R. (1994). Sources of variation in ethnographic interview data: Food avoidances in the Ituri Forest, Zaire. *Ethnology, 33,* 65-99.

Aunger, R. (1995). On ethnography: Storytelling or science? *Current Anthropology, 36,* 97-130.

Babbie, E. (1983). *The practice of social research* (3rd ed.). Belmont, CA: Wadsworth.

Bailey, K. D. (1973). Monothetic and polythetic typologies and their relation to conceptualization, measurement, and scaling. *American Sociological Review, 38,* 18-33.

Bailyn, L. (1977). Research as a cognitive process: Implications for data analysis. *Quality & Quantity, 11,* 97-117.

Barker, J. R. (1993). Tightening the iron cage: Concertive control in self-managing teams. *Administrative Science Quarterly, 38,* 408-437.

Barley, S. R. (1990). Images of imaging: Doing longitudinal field work. *Organization Science, 1,* 220-247.

Barnes, J. A. (1971). *Three styles in the study of kinship.* Berkeley: University of California Press.

Barth, F. (1989). The analysis of culture in complex societies. *Ethnos, 54,* 120-142.

Barth, F. (1995). Other knowledge and other ways of knowing. *Journal of Anthropological Research, 51,* 65-68.

Beattie, J. (1966). *Other cultures.* London: Routledge.

Becker, H. S. (1970). *Sociological work: Method and substance.* Chicago: Aldine.

Becker, H. S. (1986). *Doing things together.* Evanston, IL: Northwestern University Press.

Becker, H. S. (1990). Generalizing from case studies. In E. W. Eisner & A. Peshkin (Eds.), *Qualitative inquiry in education: The continuing debate* (pp. 233-242). New York: Teachers College Press.

Becker, H. S. (1996). The epistemology of qualitative research. In R. Jessor, A. Colby, & R. A. Shweder (Eds.), *Ethnography and human development* (pp. 53-71). Chicago: University of Chicago Press.

Becker, H. S., & Geer, B. (1960). Participant observation: The analysis of qualitative field data. In R. N. Adams & J. J. Preiss (Eds.), *Human organization research: Field relations and techniques* (pp. 267-289). Homewood, IL: Dorsey.

Becker, H. S., Geer, B., Hughes, E. C., & Strauss, A. L. (1961). *Boys in white: Student culture in medical school.* Chicago: University of Chicago Press.

Becker, H. S., Gordon, A. C., & LeBailly, R. K. (1984). Field work with the computer: Criteria for assessing systems. *Qualitative Sociology, 7,* 16-33.

Behrens, C. A. (1990). Qualitative and quantitative approaches to the analysis of anthropological data: A new synthesis. *Journal of Quantitative Anthropology, 2,* 305-328.

Beidelman, T. O. (1971). *The Kaguru: A matrilineal people of East Africa.* New York: Holt, Rinehart & Winston.

Bem, D. J. (1987). Writing the empirical journal article. In M. P. Zanna & J. M. Darley (Eds.), *The compleat academic* (pp. 171-201). New York: Random House.

Bernard, H. R. (1994). Methods belong to all of us. In R. Borofsky (Ed.), *Assessing cultural anthropology* (pp. 168-177). New York: McGraw-Hill.

Berreman, G. D. (1991). The incredible "Tasaday": Deconstructing the myth of a "stone-age" people. *Cultural Survival Quarterly, 15,* 3-45.

Birdwhistell, R. L. (1970). *Kinesics and context: Essays on body motion communication.* Philadelphia: University of Pennsylvania Press.

Bloch, M. (1991). Language, anthropology and cognitive science. *Man* (N.S.), *26,* 183-198.

Bolyanatz, A. H. (1995a). Matriliny and revisionist anthropology. *Anthropos, 90,* 169-180.

Bolyanatz, A. H. (1995b). Second reply to Watson-Franke. *Anthropos, 90,* 585-586.

Boon, J. A. (1995). Ultraobjectivity: Reading cross-culturally. In W. Natter, T. R. Schatzki, & J. P. Jones III (Eds.), *Objectivity and its other* (pp. 179-205). New York: Guilford.

Bowlin, J. R., & Stromberg, P. G. (1997). Representation and reality in the study of culture. *American Anthropologist, 99,* 123-134.

Boyle, J. S. (1994). Styles of ethnography. In J. M. Morse (Ed.), *Critical issues in qualitative research methods* (pp. 159-185). Thousand Oaks, CA: Sage.

Brennan, P. F., & Hays, B. J. (1992). The kappa statistic for establishing interrater reliability in the secondary analysis of qualitative clinical data. *Research in Nursing and Health, 15,* 153-158.

Brewer, J. D. (1994). The ethnographic critique of ethnography: Sectarianism in the RUC. *Sociology, 28,* 231-244.

Brim, J. A., & Spain, D. H. (1974). *Research design in social anthropology: Paradigms and pragmatics in the testing of hypotheses.* New York: Holt, Rinehart & Winston.

Brinberg, D., & McGrath, J. E. (1985). *Validity and the research process.* Beverly Hills, CA: Sage.

Buchanan, D., Boddy, D., & McCalman, J. (1988). Getting in, getting on, getting out, and getting back. In A. Bryman (Ed.), *Doing research in organizations* (pp. 53-67). London: Routledge.

88

Burawoy, M. (1991). The extended case method. In M. Burawoy, A. Burton, A. A. Ferguson, K. J. Fox, J. Gamson, N. Gartrell, L. Hurst, C. Kurzman, L. Salzinger, J. Schiffman, & S. Ui (Eds.), *Ethnography unbound: Power and resistance in the modern metropolis* (pp. 271-287). Berkeley: University of California Press.

Burridge, K. (1960). *Mambu: A study of Melanesian cargo movements and their social and ideological background.* New York: Harper & Row.

Campbell, D. T. (1975). Degrees of freedom and the case study. *Comparative Political Studies, 8,* 178-193.

Campion, M. A. (1993a). Are there differences between reviewers on the criteria they use to evaluate research articles? *Industrial-Organizational Psychologist, 31*(2), 29-39.

Campion, M. A. (1993b). Editorial: Article review checklist: A criterion checklist for reviewing research articles in applied psychology. *Personnel Psychology, 46,* 705-718.

Chagnon, N. A. (1968). *Yanomamo: The fierce people.* New York: Holt, Rinehart & Winston.

Cicchetti, D. V. (1991). The reliability of peer review for manuscript and grant submissions: A cross-disciplinary investigation. *Behavioral and Brain Sciences, 14,* 119-186.

Cohen, A. P. (1992). Post-fieldwork fieldwork. *Journal of Anthropological Research, 48,* 339-354.

Collier, D., & Mahon, J. E., Jr. (1993). Conceptual "stretching" revisited: Adapting categories in comparative analysis. *American Political Science Review, 87,* 845-855.

Comaroff, J., & Comaroff, J. (1992). *Ethnography and the historical imagination.* Boulder, CO: Westview.

Cooper, E. (1989). Apprenticeship as a field method: Lessons from Hong Kong. In M. W. Coy (Ed.), *Apprenticeship* (pp. 137-148). Albany: State University of New York Press.

Coy, M. W. (1989). Being what we pretend to be: The usefulness of apprenticeship as a field method. In M. W. Coy (Ed.), *Apprenticeship* (pp. 115-135). Albany: State University of New York Press.

Dalton, M. (1959). *Men who manage: Fusions of feeling and theory in administration.* New York: John Wiley.

Dalton, M. (1967). Preconceptions and methods in *Men who manage.* In P. E. Hammond (Ed.), *Sociologists at work* (pp. 58-110). Garden City, NY: Doubleday.

D'Andrade, R. (1995). Moral models in anthropology. *Current Anthropology, 36,* 399-408, 420-440.

Dauber, K. (1995). Bureaucratizing the ethnographer's magic. *Current Anthropology, 36,* 75-95.

Davis, D. L. (1993). Unintended consequences: The myth of "the return" in anthropological fieldwork. In C. B. Brettell (Ed.), *When they read what we write* (pp. 27-35). Westport, CT: Bergin & Garvey.

Davis, M. S. (1971). That's interesting! Towards a phenomenology of sociology and a sociology of phenomenology. *Philosophy of the Social Sciences, 1,* 309-344.

Dean, J. P., & Whyte, W. F. (1958). How do you know if the informant is telling the truth? *Human Organization, 17,* 34-38.

Devons, E., & Gluckman, M. (1964). Conclusion: Modes and consequences of limiting a field of study. In M. Gluckman (Ed.), *Closed systems and open minds* (pp. 158-261). Chicago: Aldine.

Doorman, F. (1991). A framework for the rapid appraisal of factors that influence the adoption and impact of new agricultural technology. *Human Organization, 50,* 235-244.

Dore, R. (1973). *British factory, Japanese factory.* Berkeley: University of California Press.

Douglas, M. (1969). Is matriliny doomed in Africa? In M. Douglas & P. M. Kaberry (Eds.), *Man in Africa* (pp. 121-136). London: Tavistock.

Dreher, M. (1994). Qualitative research methods from the reviewer's perspective. In J. M. Morse (Ed.), *Critical issues in qualitative research methods* (pp. 281-297). Thousand Oaks, CA: Sage.

Eckstein, H. (1992). Case study and theory in political science. In H. Eckstein, *Regarding politics* (pp. 117-176). Berkeley: University of California Press. (Original work published 1975)

Ellis, B. (1990). *Truth and objectivity.* Oxford: Basil Blackwell.

Ellis, C. (1995). Emotional and ethical quagmires in returning to the field. *Journal of Contemporary Ethnography, 24,* 68-98.

Elsworth, G. R. (1994). Arguing challenges to validity in field research: A realist perspective. *Knowledge: Creation, Diffusion, Utilization, 15,* 321-343.

Ember, C. R., & Ember, M. (1997). *A basic guide to cross-cultural research using the HRAF collections.* New Haven, CT:'Human Relations Area Files.

Ember, M. (1997). Evolution of the Human Relations Area Files. *Cross-Cultural Research, 31,* 3-15.

Emerson, R. M. (1987). Four ways to improve the craft of fieldwork. *Journal of Contemporary Ethnography, 16,* 69-89.

Emerson, R. M., Fretz, R. I., & Shaw, L. (1995). *Writing ethnographic fieldnotes.* Chicago: University of Chicago Press.

Emerson, R. M., & Pollner, M. (1988). On the uses of members' responses to researchers' accounts. *Human Organization, 47,* 189-198.

Ervin-Tripp, S. (1996). Context in language. In D. S. Slobin, J. Gerhardt, A. Kyratzis, & J. Guo (Eds.), *Social interaction, social context, and language* (pp. 21-36). Mahwah, NJ: Lawrence Erlbaum.

Fabian, J. (1991). Ethnographic objectivity revisited: From rigor to vigor. *Annals of Scholarship, 8,* 381-408.

Fabian, J. (1995). Ethnographic misunderstanding and the perils of context. *American Anthropologist, 97,* 41-50.

Fardon, R. (1990). Localizing strategies: The regionalization of ethnographic accounts: General introduction. In R. Fardon (Ed.), *Localizing strategies: Regional traditions of ethnographic writing* (pp. 1-35). Washington, DC: Smithsonian Institution Press.

Fine, G. A. (1993). Ten lies of ethnography: Moral dilemmas of field research. *Journal of Contemporary Ethnography, 22,* 267-294.

Firth, R. (1977). Whose frame of reference? One anthropologist's experience. *Anthropological Forum, 4,* 9-31.

Foster, G. M., Scudder, T., Colson, E., & Kemper, R. V. (1979). Conclusion: The long-term study in perspective. In G. M. Foster, T. Scudder, E. Colson, & R. V. Kemper (Eds.), *Long-term field research in social anthropology* (pp. 323-348). New York: Academic Press.

Fox, M. F. (1994). Scientific misconduct and editorial and peer review processes. *Journal of Higher Education, 65,* 298-309.

Fox, R. (1967). *Kinship and marriage: An anthropological perspective.* Harmondsworth, UK: Penguin.

Frayser, S. G. (1996). The essential tension between particularism and generalization. *Cross-Cultural Research, 30,* 291-300.

Fredericks, M., & Miller, S. I. (1997). Some brief notes on the "unfinished business" of qualitative inquiry. *Quality & Quantity, 31,* 1-13.

Garbett, K. G. (1967). The restudy as a technique for the examination of social change. In D. G. Jongmans & P. C. Gutkind (Eds.), *Anthropologists in the field* (pp. 116-132). Assen, Netherlands: Van Gorcum.

Gartrell, B. (1979). Is ethnography possible? A critique of *African Odyssey. Journal of Anthropological Research, 4,* 426-446.

90

Geertz, C. (1976). From the native's point of view. In K. H. Basso & H. A. Selby (Eds.), *Meaning in anthropology* (pp. 221-237). Albuquerque: University of New Mexico Press.

Geertz, C. (1988). *Works and lives: The anthropologist as author.* Stanford, CA: Stanford University Press.

Geertz, C. (1990). History and anthropology. *New Literary History, 21,* 321-335.

Gersick, C. J. G. (1994). Pacing strategic change: The case of a new venture. *Academy of Management Journal, 37,* 9-45.

Gerson, E. M. (1989). Computing in qualitative sociology: Data is expensive, models are cheap. *Qualitative Sociology, 12,* 411-415.

Gittelsohn, J., Shankar, A. V., West, K. P., Jr., Ram, R. M., & Gnywali, T. (1997). Estimating reactivity in direct observation studies of health behaviors. *Human Organization, 56,* 182-189.

Glaser, B. G., & Strauss, A. L. (1967). *The discovery of grounded theory: Strategies for qualitative research.* Chicago: Aldine.

Gliner, J. A. (1994). Reviewing qualitative research: Proposed criteria for fairness and rigor. *Occupational Therapy Journal of Research, 14,* 78-90.

Gluckman, M. (1961). Ethnographic data in British social anthropology. *Sociology, 9,* 5-26.

Golden-Biddle, K., & Locke, K. (1993). Appealing work: An investigation of how ethnographic texts convince. *Organization Science, 4,* 595-616.

Goodstein, D. (1991). Scientific fraud. *American Scholar, 60,* 505-515.

Gough, K. (1971). Nuer kinship: A re-examination. In T. O. Beidelman (Ed.), *The translation of culture: Essays to E. E. Evans-Pritchard* (pp. 79-121). London: Tavistock.

Gouldner, A. W. (1954). *Patterns of industrial bureaucracy: A case study of modern factory administration.* New York: Free Press.

Griffin, L. J. (1992). Temporality, events, and explanation in historical sociology: An introduction. *Sociological Methods & Research, 20,* 403-427.

Guba, E. G. (1981). Criteria for assessing the trustworthiness of naturalistic inquiries. *Educational Communication and Technology Journal, 29,* 75-92.

Gulliver, P. H. (1971). *Neighbors and networks: The idiom of kinship among the Ndendeuli of Tanzania.* Berkeley: University of California Press.

Haaland, G. (1969). Economic determinants in ethnic processes. In F. Barth (Ed.), *Ethnic groups and boundaries* (pp. 58-73). Oslo: Universitetsforlaget.

Hak, T., & Bernts, T. (1996). Coder training: Theoretical training or practical socialization? *Qualitative Sociology, 19,* 235-257.

Hammersley, M. (1990). *Reading ethnographic research: A critical guide.* London: Longman.

Hammersley, M. (1997). Qualitative data archiving: Some reflections on its prospects and problems. *Sociology, 31,* 131-142.

Hayano, D. M. (1979). Auto-ethnography. *Human Organization, 38,* 99-104.

Heider, K. G. (1988). The Rashomon effect: When ethnographers disagree. *American Anthropologist, 90,* 73-81.

Heise, D. R. (1991). Event structure analysis: A qualitative model of quantitative research. In N. G. Fielding & R. M. Lee (Eds.), *Using computers in qualitative research* (pp. 136-163). London: Sage.

Hinds, P. S., Scandrett-Hibdon, S., & McAulay, L. S. (1990). Further assessment of a method to estimate reliability and validity of qualitative research findings. *Journal of Advanced Nursing, 15,* 430-435.

Holy, L. (1986). *Strategies and norms in a changing matrilineal society.* Cambridge, UK: Cambridge University Press.

Huberman, A. M., & Miles, M. B. (1983). Drawing valid meaning from qualitative data: Some techniques of data reduction and display. *Quality & Quantity, 17,* 281-339.

Hunt, S. D. (1990). Truth in marketing theory and research. *Journal of Marketing, 54*(3), 1-15.

Hunt, S. D. (1991). *Modern marketing theory: Critical issues in the philosophy of marketing science.* Cincinnati, OH: South-Western.

Hunt, S. D. (1994). A realist theory of empirical testing: Resolving the theory-ladenness/ objectivity debate. *Philosophy of the Social Sciences, 24,* 133-158.

Jaarsma, S. R., & de Wolf, J. J. (1991). Ethnographic data-gathering: Organization and structure. *Anthropos, 86,* 385-396.

Jackson, J. E. (1990). "I am a fieldnote": Fieldnotes as a symbol of professional identity. In R. Sanjek (Ed.), *Fieldnotes: The makings of anthropology* (pp. 3-33). Ithaca, NY: Cornell University Press.

Janesick, V. J. (1994). The dance of qualitative research design: Metaphor, methodolatry, and meaning. In N. K. Denzin & Y. S. Lincoln (Eds.), *Handbook of qualitative research* (pp. 209-219). Thousand Oaks, CA: Sage.

Jenkins, T. (1994). Fieldwork and the perception of everyday life. *Man* (N.S.), *29,* 433-455.

Johnson, A. (1987). The death of ethnography: Has anthropology betrayed its mission? *The Sciences, 27*(2), 24-31.

Johnson, A., & Johnson, O. R. (1990). Quality into quantity: On the measurement potential of ethnographic fieldnotes. In R. Sanjek (Ed.), *Fieldnotes: The makings of anthropology* (pp. 161-186). Ithaca, NY: Cornell University Press.

Johnson, J. C. (1990). *Selecting ethnographic informants.* Newbury Park, CA: Sage.

Kapferer, B. (1972). *Strategy and transaction in an African factory: African workers and Indian management in a Zambian town.* Manchester, UK: Manchester University Press.

Katz, J. (1983). A theory of qualitative methodology: The social system of analytic fieldwork. In R. M. Emerson (Ed.), *Contemporary field research* (pp. 127-148). Boston: Little, Brown.

Katz, J. (1997). Ethnography's warrants. *Sociological Methods & Research, 25,* 391-423.

Keane, W. (1997). Knowing one's place: National language and the idea of the local in Eastern Indonesia. *Cultural Anthropology, 12,* 37-63.

Keesing, R. M. (1987). Anthropology as interpretive quest. *Current Anthropology, 28,* 161-176.

Kidder, L. H. (1981). Qualitative research and quasi-experimental frameworks. In M. B. Brewer & B. E. Collins (Eds.), *Scientific inquiry and the social sciences* (pp. 226-256). San Francisco: Jossey-Bass.

Kirchgassler, K. U. (1991). Validity: The quest for reality in quantitative and qualitative research. *Quality & Quantity, 25,* 285-295.

Kirk, J., & Miller, M. L. (1986). *Reliability and validity in qualitative research.* Beverly Hills, CA: Sage.

Kleinman, S., Stenross, B., & McMahon, M. (1994). Privileging fieldwork over interviews: Consequences for identity and practice. *Symbolic Interaction, 17,* 37-50.

Kondo, D. K. (1990). *Crafting selves: Power, gender, and discourses of identity in a Japanese workplace.* Chicago: University of Chicago Press.

Kritzer, H. M. (1994). Interpretation and validity assessment in qualitative research: The case of H. W. Perry's *Deciding to decide. Law & Social Inquiry, 19,* 687-724.

Lave, J., & Wenger, E. (1991). *Situated learning: Legitimate peripheral participation.* Cambridge, UK: Cambridge University Press.

Leach, E. R. (1954). *Political systems of Highland Burma.* London: University of London, Athlone Press.

Leach, E. R. (1961). *Rethinking anthropology.* London: University of London, Athlone Press.

Learned, K. E. (1995). *The creation of firm resources: A native ethnography.* Unpublished doctoral dissertation, Texas Tech University.

Learned, K. E., & Stewart, A. (1994). *Opportunistic participation in management research.* Presentation at the Symposium on Challenges in Conducting Field Research on Firm-Level Entrepreneurship, conducted at the annual meeting of the National Academy of Management.

LeCompte, M. D., & Preissle, J. (1993). *Ethnography and qualitative design in educational research* (2nd ed.). San Diego, CA: Academic Press.

Lee, R. M. (1995). *Dangerous fieldwork*. Thousand Oaks, CA: Sage.

Leininger, M. (1994). Evaluation criteria and critique of qualitative research studies. In J. M. Morse (Eds.), *Critical issues in qualitative research methods* (pp. 95-115). Thousand Oaks, CA: Sage.

Leonard-Barton, D. (1990). A dual methodology for case studies: Synergistic use of a longitudinal single site with replicated multiple studies. *Organization Science, 1,* 248-266.

LeVine, R. A. (1981). Knowledge and fallibility in anthropological field research. In M. B. Brewer & B. E. Collins (Eds.), *Scientific inquiry and the social sciences* (pp. 172-193). San Francisco: Jossey-Bass.

Lewis, I. M. (Ed.). (1968). *History and social anthropology*. London: Tavistock.

Lewis, I. M. (1976). *Social anthropology in perspective*. Harmondsworth, UK: Penguin.

Lincoln, Y. S., & Denzin, N. K. (1994). The fifth moment. In N. K. Denzin & Y. S. Lincoln (Eds.), *Handbook of qualitative research* (pp. 575-586). Thousand Oaks, CA: Sage.

Lincoln, Y. S., & Guba, E. G. (1985). *Naturalistic inquiry*. Beverly Hills, CA: Sage.

Lincoln, Y. S., & Guba, E. G. (1986). But is it rigorous? Trustworthiness and authenticity in naturalistic evaluation. In D. D. Williams (Ed.), *Naturalistic evaluation* (pp. 73-84). San Francisco: Jossey-Bass.

Lincoln, Y. S., & Guba, E. G. (1990). Judging the quality of case study reports. *International Journal of Qualitative Studies in Education, 3,* 53-59.

Locke, K. (1996). Rewriting *The Discovery of Grounded Theory* after 25 years? *Journal of Management Inquiry, 5,* 239-245.

Lofland, J. (1995). Analytic ethnography: Features, failings, and futures. *Journal of Contemporary Ethnography, 24,* 30-67.

Lofland, J., & Lofland, L. H. (1995). *Analyzing social settings: A guide to qualitative observation and analysis* (3rd ed.). Belmont, CA: Wadsworth.

Louis, M. R., & Bartunek, J. M. (1992). Insider/outsider research teams: Collaboration across diverse perspectives. *Journal of Management Inquiry, 1,* 101-110.

Lutkehaus, N. (1990). Refractions of reality: On the use of other ethnographers' fieldnotes. In R. Sanjek (Ed.), *Fieldnotes: The makings of anthropology* (pp. 303-323). Ithaca, NY: Cornell University Press.

Lyon, E. (1997). Applying ethnography. *Journal of Contemporary Ethnography, 26,* 3-27.

Mahmood, C. K., & Armstrong, S. L. (1992). Do ethnic groups exist? A cognitive perspective on the concept of cultures. *Ethnology, 31,* 1-14.

Malinowski, B. (1961). *Argonauts of the western Pacific*. New York: Dutton. (Original work published 1922)

Mandel, S. W. (1996). *Organization taxonomy: Searching for performance while solving the problems of polythetic classification*. Unpublished doctoral dissertation, Texas Tech University.

March, J. G., Sproull, L. S., & Tamuz, M. (1991). Learning from samples of one or fewer. *Organization Science, 2,* 1-13.

Markus, M. L. (1992). *Writing up "intensive" research in the "standard article format": Enablement or constraint?* Unpublished manuscript, Claremont Graduate School, Programs in Information Science.

Maxwell, J. A. (1992). Understanding and validity in qualitative research. *Harvard Educational Review, 62,* 279-300.

Mayer, A. C. (1989). Anthropological memories. *Man* (N.S.), *24,* 203-218.

McCracken, G. (1988). *The long interview*. Newbury Park, CA: Sage.

McKelvey, B. (1982). *Organizational systematics: Taxonomy, evolution, classification.* Berkeley: University of California Press.

Megill, A. (1994). Introduction: Four senses of objectivity. In A. Megill (Ed.), *Rethinking objectivity* (pp. 1-20). Durham, NC: Duke University Press.

Miles, M. B., & Huberman, A. M. (1984). *Qualitative data analysis: A sourcebook of new methods.* Beverly Hills, CA: Sage.

Miles, M. B., & Huberman, A. M. (1994). *Qualitative data analysis: An expanded sourcebook* (2nd ed.). Thousand Oaks, CA: Sage.

Miller, D., & Friesen, P. H. (1984). *Organizations: A quantum view.* Englewood Cliffs, NJ: Prentice Hall.

Miller, C. W. (1940). Methodological consequences of the sociology of knowledge. *American Journal of Sociology, 46,* 316-330.

Miner, H. (1956). Body ritual among the Nacirema. *American Anthropologist, 58,* 503-507.

Mitchell, J. C. (1974). Case and situational analysis. *Sociological Review, 31,* 187-211.

Monge, P. R. (1990). Theoretical and analytical issues in studying organizational processes. *Organization Science, 1,* 406-430.

Moran, E. F. (1995). Introduction: Norms for ethnographic reporting. In E. F. Moran (Ed.), *The comparative analysis of human societies* (pp. 1-20). Boulder, CO: Lynne Rienner.

Morgan, D. L. (1988). *Focus groups as qualitative research.* Newbury Park, CA: Sage.

Morse, E. A. (1998). *The temporal dynamics of firm resource creation: An event structure analysis in an entrepreneurial firm.* Unpublished doctoral dissertation, Texas Tech University.

Morse, J. M. (1994). "Emerging from the data": The cognitive processes of analysis in qualitative research. In J. M. Morse (Ed.), *Critical issues in qualitative research methods* (pp. 23-43). Thousand Oaks, CA: Sage.

Muecke, M. A. (1994). On the evaluation of ethnographies. In J. M. Morse (Ed.), *Critical issues in qualitative research methods* (pp. 187-209). Thousand Oaks, CA: Sage.

Murdock, G. P., Ford, C. S., Hudson, A. E., Kennedy, R., Simmons, L. W., & Whiting, J. W. M. (1987). *Outline of cultural materials* (5th rev. ed.). New Haven, CT: Human Relations Area Files.

Nachman, S. R. (1984). Lies my informant told me. *Journal of Anthropological Research, 40,* 536-555.

Nader, L. (1976). Professional standards and what we study. In M. A. Rynkiewich & J. P. Spradley (Eds.), *Ethics and anthropology* (pp. 167-182). New York: John Wiley.

Naroll, R. (1970a). Data quality control in cross-cultural surveys. In R. Naroll & R. Cohen (Eds.), *A handbook of method in cultural anthropology* (pp. 927-945). Garden City, NY: Natural History Press.

Naroll, R. (1970b). What have we learned from cross-cultural surveys? *American Anthropologist, 72,* 1227-1288.

Needham, R. (1975). Polythetic classification: Convergence and consequences. *Man* (N.S.), *10,* 349-369.

Noblit, G. W., & Hare, R. D. (1988). *Meta-ethnography: Synthesizing qualitative studies.* Newbury Park, CA: Sage.

Obligacion, F. R. (1994). Managing perceived deception among respondents: A traveler's tale. *Journal of Contemporary Ethnography, 23,* 29-50.

Oppong, C. (1974). *Marriage among a matrilineal elite.* Cambridge, UK: Cambridge University Press.

Ottenberg, S. (1987). Return to the field: Anthropological *deja vu. Cambridge Anthropology, 923,* 16-31.

Ottenberg, S. (1990). Thirty years of fieldnotes: Changing relationships to the text. In R. Sanjek (Ed.), *Fieldnotes: The makings of anthropology* (pp. 139-160). Ithaca, NY: Cornell University Press.

Ottenberg, S. (1994). Changes over time in an African culture and in an anthropologist. In D. D. Fowler & D. L. Hardesty (Eds.), *Others knowing others: Perspectives on ethnographic careers* (pp. 91-118). Washington, DC: Smithsonian Institution Press.

Parmentier, R. J. (1994). *Signs in society: Studies in semiotic anthropology*. Bloomington: Indiana University Press.

Pettigrew, A. M. (1990). Longitudinal field research on change: Theory and practice. *Organization Science, 1,* 267-292.

Plath, D. W. (1990). Fieldnotes, filed notes, and the conferring of note. In R. Sanjek (Ed.), *Fieldnotes: The makings of anthropology* (pp. 371-384). Ithaca, NY: Cornell University Press.

Punch, M. (1986). *The politics and ethics of fieldwork*. Beverly Hills, CA: Sage.

Rabinow, P. (1977). *Reflections on fieldwork in Morocco*. Berkeley: University of California Press.

Ragin, C. C. (1987). *The comparative method*. Berkeley: University of California Press.

Rescher, N. (1997). *Objectivity: The obligations of impersonal reason*. Notre Dame, IN: University of Notre Dame Press.

Reyna, S. P. (1994). Literary anthropology and the case against science. *Man* (N.S.), *29,* 555-581.

Richards, A. I. (1950). Some types of family structure amongst the central Bantu. In A. R. Radcliffe-Brown & D. Forde (Eds.), *African systems of kinship and marriage* (pp. 207-251). London: Oxford University Press.

Richards, T. J., & Richards, L. (1994). Using computers in qualitative research. In N. K. Denzin & Y. S. Lincoln (Eds.), *Handbook of qualitative research* (pp. 445-462). Thousand Oaks, CA: Sage.

Riemer, J. W. (1977). Varieties of opportunistic research. *Urban Life, 5,* 467-477.

Rodgers, B. L., & Cowles, K. V. (1993). The qualitative research audit trail: A complex collection of documentation. *Research in Nursing and Health, 16,* 219-226.

Rosen, M. (1991). Coming to terms with the field: Understanding and doing organizational ethnography. *Journal of Management Studies, 28,* 1-24.

Rosenblatt, P. C. (1981). Ethnographic case studies. In M. B. Brewer & B. E. Collins (Eds.), *Scientific inquiry and the social sciences* (pp. 194-225). San Francisco: Jossey-Bass.

Rothstein, H. R. (1990). Interrater reliability of job performance ratings: Growth to asymptote level with increasing opportunity to observe. *Journal of Applied Psychology, 75,* 322-327.

Royal Anthropological Institute of Great Britain and Ireland. (1951). *Notes and queries on anthropology* (6th ed.). London: Routledge & Kegan Paul.

Rudie, I. (1994). Making sense of new experience. In K. Hastrup & P. Hervik (Eds.), *Social experience and anthropological knowledge* (pp. 28-44). London: Routledge.

Sahlins, M. (1961). The segmentary lineage: An organization of predatory expansion. *American Anthropologist, 63,* 322-343.

Sanjek, R. (1990a). On ethnographic validity. In R. Sanjek (Ed.), *Fieldnotes: The makings of anthropology* (pp. 385-418). Ithaca, NY: Cornell University Press.

Sanjek, R. (1990b). The secret life of fieldnotes. In R. Sanjek (Ed.), *Fieldnotes: The makings of anthropology* (pp. 187-270). Ithaca, NY: Cornell University Press.

Sanjek, R. (1991). The ethnographic present. *Man* (N.S.), *26,* 609-628.

Sartori, G. (1970). Concept misformation in comparative politics. *American Political Science Review, 64,* 1033-1053.

Sayles, L. R., & Stewart, A. (1995). Belated recognition for work-flow entrepreneurs: A case of selective perception and amnesia in management thought. *Entrepreneurship Theory and Practice, 19*(3), 7-23.

Scarce, R. (1994). No trial but tribulations: When courts and ethnography conflict. *Journal of Contemporary Ethnography, 23,* 123-149.

Schensul, S. L. (1993). Using Ethnograph to build a survey instrument. *Cultural Anthropology Methods, 52,* 9.

Scheper-Hughes, N. (1995). The primacy of the ethical: Propositions for a militant anthropology. *Current Anthropology, 36,* 409-440.

Schlegel, A. (1972). *Male dominance and female autonomy: Domestic authority in matrilineal societies.* New Haven, CT: Human Relations Area Files.

Schneider, D. M. (1961). Introduction: The distinctive features of matrilineal descent groups. In D. M. Schneider & K. Gough (Eds.), *Matrilineal kinship* (pp. 1-29). Berkeley: University of California Press.

Schofield, J. W. (1990). Increasing the generalizability of qualitative research. In E. W. Eisner & A. Peshkin (Eds.), *Qualitative inquiry in education: The continuing debate* (pp. 201-232). New York: Teachers College Press.

Schwandt, T. A., & Halpern, E. S. (1988). *Linking auditing and metaevaluation: Enhancing quality in applied research.* Newbury Park, CA: Sage.

Schwartzman, H. B. (1993). *Ethnography in organizations.* Newbury Park, CA: Sage.

Searle, J. R. (1995). *The construction of social reality.* New York: Free Press.

Seidel, J., & Kelle, U. (1995). Different functions of coding in the analysis of textual data. In U. Kelle (Ed.), *Computer-aided qualitative data analysis* (pp. 52-61). London: Sage.

Seidel, J. V., Kjolseth, R., & Seymour, E. (1988). *The Ethnograph: A user's guide, version 3.0.* Corvallis, OR: Qualis Research Associates.

Shulman, D. (1994). Dirty data and investigative methods: Some lessons from private detective work. *Journal of Contemporary Ethnography, 23,* 214-253.

Silverman, D. (1993). *Interpreting qualitative data.* London: Sage.

Smith, J. K. (1984). The problem of criteria for judging interpretive inquiry. *Educational Evaluation and Policy Analysis, 6,* 379-391.

Smith, R. J. (1990). Hearing voices, joining the chorus: Appropriating someone else's fieldnotes. In R. Sanjek (Ed.), *Fieldnotes: The makings of anthropology* (pp. 356-370). Ithaca, NY: Cornell University Press.

Stern, P. N. (1994). Eroding grounded theory. In J. M. Morse (Ed.), *Critical issues in qualitative research methods* (pp. 212-223). Thousand Oaks, CA: Sage.

Stewart, A. (1989). *Team entrepreneurship.* Newbury Park, CA: Sage.

Stewart, A. (1990). The Bigman metaphor for entrepreneurship: A "library tale" with morals on alternatives for further research. *Organization Science, 1,* 143-159.

Stewart, A. (1995). Journal ranking in Nacirema ritual: The case of I. C. MacMillan's publishing "forums." *Advances in Strategic Management, 11*(A), 3-37.

Stewart, A., & Krackhardt, D. (1997). *Pinky's puppies: Structural spanning and resource creation in entrepreneurship.* Paper presented at the annual meeting of the National Academy of Management.

Stewart, A., Learned, K. E., Mandel, S. W., & Peterson, K. M. (1995). Using field research on firm-level entrepreneurship: A coda. *Entrepreneurship Theory and Practice, 19*(3), 175-184.

Stocking, G. W., Jr. (1992). *The ethnographer's magic and other essays in the history of anthropology.* Madison: University of Wisconsin Press.

Stoller, P. (1994). Ethnographies as texts/ethnographers as griots. *American Ethnologist, 21,* 353-366.

Strathern, M. (1987). Out of context: The persuasive fictions of anthropology. *Current Anthropology, 28,* 251-281.

Strathern, M. (1992). Parts and wholes: Refiguring relationships in a post-plural world. In A. Kuper (Ed.), *Conceptualizing society* (pp. 75-104). London: Routledge.

Strauss, A. L. (1987). *Qualitative analysis for social scientists*. New York: Cambridge University Press.

Strauss, A. L., & Corbin, J. (1990). *Basics of qualitative research: Grounded theory procedures and techniques*. Newbury Park, CA: Sage.

Strauss, A. L., Fagerhaugh, S., Suczek, B., & Wiener, C. (1985). *Social organization of medical work*. Chicago: University of Chicago Press.

Sutton, R. I. (1997). The virtues of closet qualitative research. *Organization Science, 8,* 97-106.

Tedlock, B. (1991). From participant observation to the observation of participation: The emergence of narrative ethnography. *Journal of Anthropological Research, 47,* 69-94.

Tesch, R. (1990). *Qualitative research: Analysis types and software tools*. Philadelphia: Falmer.

Thornton, R. (1988). The rhetoric of ethnographic holism. *Cultural Anthropology, 3,* 285-303.

Tobias, P. V. (1994). Piltdown unmasked. *The Sciences, 34*(1), 38-43.

Trotter, R. T. (1991). Ethnographic research methods for applied medical anthropology. In C. E. Hill (Ed.), *Training manual in applied medical anthropology* (pp. 180-212). Washington, DC: American Anthropological Association.

Turner, V. W. (1957). *Schism and continuity in an African society*. Manchester, UK: Manchester University Press.

Ulrich, D., & McKelvey, B. (1990). General organizational classification: An empirical test using the United States and Japan. *Organization Science, 1,* 99-118.

Van Maanen, J. (1983). The moral fix: On the ethics of fieldwork. In R. M. Emerson (Ed.), *Contemporary field research* (pp. 269-287). Boston: Little, Brown.

Van Maanen, J. (1988). *Tales of the field: On writing ethnography*. Chicago: University of Chicago Press.

Van Maanen, J. (1991). Playing back the tape: Early days in the field. In W. B. Shaffir & R. A. Stebbins (Eds.), *Experiencing fieldwork* (pp. 31-42). Newbury Park, CA: Sage.

Van Maanen, J. (1995). Trade secrets: On writing ethnography. In R. H. Brown (Ed.), *Postmodern representations* (pp. 60-79). Urbana: University of Illinois Press.

Van Velsen, J. (1964). *The politics of kinship: A study in social manipulation among the lakeside Tonga*. Manchester, UK: Manchester University Press.

Van Velsen, J. (1967). The extended-case method and situational analysis. In A. L. Epstein (Ed.), *The craft of social anthropology* (pp. 129-149). London: Tavistock.

Wallendorf, M., & Belk, R. W. (1989). Assessing trustworthiness in naturalistic consumer research. In E. C. Hirschman (Ed.), *Interpretive consumer research* (pp. 69-84). Provo, UT: Association for Consumer Research.

Watson-Franke, M.-B. (1992). Masculinity and the "matrilineal puzzle." *Anthropos, 87,* 475-488.

Watson-Franke, M.-B. (1995). Revisionism or the recovery of matrilineal women's centrality? A reply to Bolyanatz. *Anthropos, 90,* 582-585.

Weick, K. E. (1979). *The social psychology of organizing*. Reading, MA: Addison-Wesley.

Werner, O., & Bernard, H. R. (1994). Ethnographic sampling. *Cultural Anthropology Methods, 62,* 7-9.

Werner, O., & Schoepfle, G. M. (1987). *Systematic fieldwork* (2 vols.). Newbury Park, CA: Sage.

White, D. (1990). Reliability in comparative and ethnographic observations: The example of high inference father-child interaction measures. *Journal of Quantitative Anthropology, 2,* 109-150.

Whyte, W. F. (1948). *Human relations in the restaurant industry*. New York: McGraw-Hill.

Whyte, W. F., with Whyte, K. K. (1984). *Learning from the field: A guide from experience*. Beverly Hills, CA: Sage.

Whyte, W. F. (1993). *Street corner society: The social structure of an Italian slum* (4th ed.). Chicago: University of Chicago Press.

Wiewel, W., & Hunter, A. (1985). The interorganizational network as a resource: A comparative case study on organizational genesis. *Administrative Science Quarterly, 30,* 482-496.

Wikan, U. (1991). Toward an experience-near anthropology. *Cultural Anthropology, 6,* 285-305.

Wolcott, H. F. (1990a). Making a study "more ethnographic." *Journal of Contemporary Ethnography, 19,* 44-72.

Wolcott, H. F. (1990b). *Writing up qualitative research.* Newbury Park, CA: Sage.

Wolcott, H. F. (1992). Posturing in qualitative inquiry. In M. D. LeCompte, W. L. Millroy, & J. Preissle (Eds.), *The handbook of qualitative research in education* (pp. 3-52). New York: Academic Press.

Wolcott, H. F. (1994). *Transforming qualitative data.* Thousand Oaks, CA: Sage.

Yin, R. K. (1984). *Case study research: Design and methods.* Beverly Hills, CA: Sage.

ABOUT THE AUTHOR

ALEX STEWART is Associate Professor of Management and Director of the Center for Entrepreneurial and Family Business at Texas Tech University. His past interests are probably apparent from his brazen self-citations, but his background may be less discernible: B.A. and M.A. in social anthropology, Ph.D. in political science with a minor in social anthropology, and M.B.A. while ABD, all from York University in Toronto. His future interests are occasions for his biographical imagination. Let's say that he might find work on entrepreneurial Japanese kinship-oriented business enticing—but in Lubbock? Currently, he is occupied with new books, one tentatively titled *Crafting Entrepreneurial Organizations: Ten Takes on Entrepreneurial Organizing,* the other (with Kevin Learned as lead author) tentatively titled *Creating Capabilities: A Native Ethnography of an Entrepreneurial Firm.*

Qualitative Research Methods

Series Editor
JOHN VAN MAANEN
Massachusetts Institute of Technology

Associate Editors:
Peter K. Manning, *Michigan State University*
& Marc L. Miller, *University of Washington*

Other volumes in this series listed on outside back cover